🌱 DEPAUL UNIVERSITY

Chicago, IL

Department of

Writing, Rhetoric, & Discourse

Master of Arts Degrees in

* New Media Studies
* Writing, Rhetoric, & Discourse

with concentrations in

Professional & Technical Writing
Teaching Writing & Language

Faculty

Matthew Abraham
Julie Bokser
Darsie Bowden
Antonio Ceraso
René De los Santos
Lisa Dush
Shaun Slattery
Christine Tardy
Peter Vandenberg

las.depaul.edu/wrd

wrd

Reviewers

All essay submissions are reviewed blind by two external readers; those listed below are members of the active reader pool. We thank them for their critical contributions to scholarship in the field.

Linda Adler-Kassner
Tom Amorose
Valerie Balester
Cheryl Ball
Patricia Belanoff
Patricia Bizzell
Bill Bolin
Darsie Bowden
Robert Brooke
Nancy Buffington
Beth Burmester
Paul Butler
MaryAnn Cain
Carol Clark
Jennifer Clary-Lemon
Lisa Coleman
James Comas
Juanita Rodgers Comfort
Thomas Deans
Jane Detweiler
Ronda Leathers Dively
Sidney Dobrin
Kim Donehower
Donna Dunbar-Odom
Lynnell Edwards
Janet Carey Eldred
Michele Eodice
Heidi Estrem
Sheryl Fontaine
Helen Fox
Tom Fox
Christy Friend
Cathy Gabor

Lynée Lewis Gaillet
Alice Gilliam
Maureen Daly Goggin
Angela González
Lorie Goodman
Heather Brodie Graves
Roger Graves
Paul Hanstedt
Dana Harrington
Cynthia Haynes
Paul Heilker
Carl Herndl
Anne Herrington
Brooke Hessler
Charlotte Hogg
Bruce Horner
Rebecca Moore Howard
Sue Hum
Brian Huot
Asao Inoue
Rebecca Jackson
T. R. Johnson
Martha Kruse
bonnie kyburz
Mary Lamb
Joe Law
Donna LeCourt
Neal Lerner
Carrie Leverenz
Drew Loewe
Min-Zhan Lu
Tim Mayers

Lisa McClure
Dan Meltzer
Laura Rose Micciche
Susan Miller
Clyde Moneyhun
Roxanne Mountford
Gerald P. Mulderig
Joan A. Mullin
Joddy Murray
Marshall Myers
Gerald Nelms
Jon Olson
Peggy O'Neill
Derek Owens
Irvin Peckham
Donna Qualley
Ellen Quandahl
Kelly Ritter
Randall Roorda
Blake Scott
Ellen Schendel
Carol Severino
Wendy Sharer
Steve Sherwood
Donna Strickland
Jennifer Trainor
Peter Vandenberg
Deirdre Vinyard
Kathleen Welch
Katherine Wills
Rosemary Winslow
Janet Zepernick

CELJ

Member of the Council of Editors of Learned Journals

composition STUDIES

Volume 38, Number 1

Spring 2010

TCU

Texas Christian University
www.compositionstudies.tcu.edu

SUBSCRIPTIONS

Composition Studies is published twice each year (May and November). Subscription rates: Individuals $25 (Domestic) and $30 (International); Institutions $75 (Domestic) and $75 (International); Students $15.

BACK ISSUES

Some back issues are available at $8 per issue. Photocopies of earlier issues are available for $3.

BOOK REVIEWS

Assignments are made from a file of potential book reviewers. To have your name added to the file, send a current vita to the Book Review Editor at asao@inoueweb.com.

SUBMISSIONS

All appropriate essay submissions will be blind reviewed by two external readers. Manuscripts should be 3,500-7,500 words and conform to current MLA guidelines for format and documentation; they should be free of author's names and other identifying references. *Electronic submissions are preferred*: consult our web site for details. (For print submissions, submit three titled, letter-quality copies with a cover letter including the title and author contact information, loose postage sufficient to mail manuscripts to two reviewers, and a #10 SASE for the return of reviewer comments.) *Composition Studies* will not consider previously published manuscripts. We discourage the submission of conference papers that have not been revised or extended for a critical reading audience. Those wishing to submit Course Designs should first consult our web site for specific instructions. Letters to the editor and responses to articles are strongly encouraged.

Direct all correspondence to:

Jennifer Clary-Lemon, Editor
Department of Rhetoric, Writing, and Communications
University of Winnipeg
515 Portage Avenue Winnipeg, MB R3B 2E9
Canada

Composition Studies is grateful for the generous support of the Department of English and the AddRan College of Liberal Arts at TCU.

© Copyright 2010 by Brad E. Lucas, Editor
Printing managed by Parlor Press, www.parlorpress.com
ISSN 1534-9322

www.compositionstudies.tcu.edu

composition STUDIES

Volume 38, Number 1

Spring 2010

BOOK REVIEWS

EDITOR'S NOTE

This is my last issue as Editor of *Composition Studies*, and it is with great pleasure that I introduce the new editorial team for *Composition Studies*: Editor Jennifer Clary-Lemon (University of Winnipeg) and Book Review Editor Asao Inoue (California State University, Fresno). After an extensive review process that began with nominations from our Advisory Board, and ended with a short-list of exceptional candidates, Clary-Lemon was elected to provide leadership for the journal and establish its new home in Winnepeg, Manitoba, 1300 miles north of Fort Worth, Texas.

Jennifer Clary-Lemon is assistant professor of rhetoric at the University of Winnipeg. She is pleased to be returning to Composition Studies as Editor ten years after beginning her scholarly career as an editorial assistant for the journal under the editorship of Peter Vandenberg. Her research and teaching interests include composition history and disciplinarity, as well as the rhetorics of representation. Recent publications can be found in *College Composition and Communication*, *Discourse and Society*, and the *American Review of Canadian Studies*.

Asao B. Inoue is the Assessment Expert for the College of Arts and Humanities and Co-Director of First Year Writing at California State University, Fresno. He has published numerous articles and chapters on classroom and large-scale writing assessment, particularly validity and the ways racial formations may be accounted for in writing assessments. His current projects include a manuscript that investigates racial formations and racism in various writing assessment technologies, and a co-edited collection (with Mya Poe) on writing assessment and racial formations and racism.

Composition Studies 38.1 (2010) / ISSN 1534-9322

Since *Composition Studies* returned to its TCU birthplace in 2003, it has become a self-sustaining publication with operating bylaws that ensure the journal will have longevity and oversight in the decades to come. It has been a pleasure to co-edit the journal with my colleagues Ann George and Carrie Leverenz, along with a series of Managing Editors that kept our operations running smoothly: Liz Weiser, Erin Sagerson, Angela Gonzalez, Drew Loewe, Amy Milakovic, Kristi Serrano, and David Elder. We have enjoyed the process of publishing timely scholarship, pedagogical designs, reviews of new books, and occasional features like interviews, national survey data, essays, and special editions on "Composition in the Small College" and "The Writing Major."

In this issue, we include articles about the ubiquitous but neglected slide presentation; a rethinking of teaching genre by familiar example; and the role of collecting, memory, and literacy. Also included is an analysis of discursive strategies in an environmental debate and a study about the issue of participation in the composition classroom. Following a course design centered on blogging, you can read an essay by former *Composition Studies* editor Bob Mayberry, who reflects on his experiences as an undergraduate who found his own path to teaching and followed it—and in the process commemorates the fortieth anniversary of the Kent State shootings on May 4, 1970. Indeed, Uncle Paul weaves on.

Brad E. Lucas

An Inconvenient Tool:
Rethinking the Role of Slideware in the Writing Classroom

Laurie E. Gries and Collin Gifford Brooke

Every so often, a technology will saturate the market to the extent that the name of the product becomes a stand-in for the technology itself, like Kleenex or Xerox. While it belongs to the broader genre of slideware,[1] Microsoft PowerPoint is perhaps the best example of software that has achieved that level of ubiquity. Despite Apple's Keynote, the Presentation Editor within Google Docs, Zoho Show, and others, the visual display of sequential slides (most typically during an oral presentation) has become synonymous with PowerPoint. Although it has achieved this level of popularity, PowerPoint is also considered by many to be synonymous with mind-numbing boredom, painful expository bullet points, and the overexposure of the Microsoft clip art library. That is, PowerPoint may be used widely, but it is just as widely disparaged, and often used only begrudgingly. For all of the success PowerPoint has achieved as a piece of software, it has inspired an equal amount of dismay in dimly lit classrooms, boardrooms, and conferences across the world.

To imagine, then, that a PowerPoint presentation might win an Academy Award sounds absurd, like someone receiving a Pulitzer Prize for a five-paragraph theme. And yet, in 2007, *An Inconvenient Truth*, the documentary based upon Al Gore's slideshow about global warming, received two Academy Awards (for best documentary and best original song). By the time the film was released, Gore himself estimated that he had delivered his presentation more than a thousand times; combined with the worldwide success of the documentary, this suggests that millions of people have seen this single slideshow, and presumably acted upon the message it was designed to support. Nancy Duarte explains in *slide:ology* that Gore "has done more than any other individual to legitimize multimedia presentations as one of the most compelling communication vehicles on the planet" (86). While the rehabilitation of slideware may seem a negligible benefit when compared to the political and environmental impact of *Inconvenient Truth*, we would argue that the success of Gore's documentary is merely the most visible example of a larger movement towards a re-legitimation of PowerPoint and slideware more broadly. This movement has emerged, in part, by redefining the terms according to which we think about multimedia presentations. As we discuss below, PowerPoint has been articulated as an inferior information technology, incapable of the kind of information density possible with other media. Industry professionals like Duarte and Garr Reynolds, however, refuse to engage this critique of PowerPoint on those terms, seeing it instead as a rich environment for the practice of multimedia rhetoric, as opposed to information delivery.

In rhetoric and composition, we are more likely to hold to the former position, seeing slideware as a necessary evil at best. Although we in the academy hold different goals and motives, our opinions of presentation software have generally run parallel to those of the business world. It is time that we reconsider our received opinions regarding slideware, and listen closely to the new voices (and visions) of presentation and design experts. After all, some of the leading thinkers in technology-related fields, such as Lawrence Lessig and Steve Jobs, are among slideware's most dynamic presenters. Others such as Daniel Pink are encouraging us to make more room for creativity in our thinking, suggesting that critiques of PowerPoint may not provide us with the whole story when it comes to considering slideware. We argue below that when used in dynamic, inventive ways, slideware can become an integral and productive part of our pedagogical and technological repertoires. We believe it is time to set aside our mistrust and disdain for software like PowerPoint and consider carefully how it might aid us in the teaching of writing. Using the presentation format Pecha Kucha as a model, we offer productive reasons and ways to reconfigure the role of slideware in the composing process. Slideware design and delivery can play a creative and inventive role in our students' making of writing.

The Rise and Fall (and Rise?) of PowerPoint

Because we have generally accepted the terms of the PowerPoint "debate" as it has played out in public discourse—going so far sometimes as to teach Edward Tufte's and others' critiques of the software—it is worth reviewing that debate, and understanding the values implied there, before we explore slideware's specific application in the classroom. Understanding how professionals like Reynolds and Duarte are positioning slideware can provide us with useful guidance as we consider it for adoption.

In part, the return to slideware is a response to the public backlash against PowerPoint that followed its meteoric rise to popularity. In a 2001 *New Yorker* article titled "Absolute PowerPoint," for example, Ian Parker claimed that PowerPoint "is software you impose on other people" (76). Parker details PowerPoint's success, its presence at the confluence of factors like the changing structure of industry in the 1960s and 1970s, the emergence of affordable personal computers in the 1980s, and the fear that most people have of public speaking. "Because PowerPoint can be an impressive antidote to fear," Parker explains, "there seems to be no great impulse to fight th[e] influence" of PowerPoint itself, or of the templates supplied with the program (78). There is an unevenness to Parker's treatment of PowerPoint in the article, however—an uncertainty about whether or not the ubiquity of PowerPoint is worth taking seriously. On the one hand, he explains that PowerPoint

> has a private, interior influence. It edits ideas. It is, almost surreptitious-ly, a business manual as well as a business suit, with an opinion—an oddly pedantic, prescriptive opinion—about the way we should think. It helps you make a case, but it also makes its own case: about how to organize information, how much information to organize, how to look at the world. (76)

Implied in Parker's more serious descriptions is the question of whether any software should play as large a role as PowerPoint seems to in the shaping of our ideas. And yet this question alternates throughout with amused accounts of the "joke" of the Auto-Content Wizard, product de-velopment being driven by marketing departments, a housewife driving her children to tears with slideshows about "domestic harmony," and the infamous PowerPoint translation-parody of the Gettysburg Address. Despite both anecdotal and empirical evidence of PowerPoint's effect on informa-tion and subsequent audience judgments, one has the impression from Parker that to take PowerPoint too seriously would result in becoming the anonymous user who admits "I caught myself planning out (in my head) the slides I would need to explain to my wife why we couldn't afford a vacation this year" (78).

If there is some ambivalence to Parker's account of PowerPoint, there is none in Edward Tufte's scathing critique of the software, his 2003, self-published essay, "The Cognitive Style of PowerPoint: Pitching Out Corrupts Within." The cover visual for his essay is instructive: Tufte adds several thought and speech balloons to a picture of Stalin Square in Budapest, with comments like, "There's no bullet list like Stalin's bullet list!" and "For re-education campaigns, nothing is better than the Auto-Content Wizard!" The humor of these additions is strained at best; underlying it is a strong sense of disapproval, if not outright contempt, for PowerPoint, and the core of Tufte's argument is deadly serious. In what is perhaps the conceptual centerpiece of the essay, Tufte places on two facing pages a single slide from the NASA slideshow that preceded the 2003 explosion of the space shuttle Columbia. The slide is surrounded by several paragraphs of Tufte's detailed commentary critiquing the "festival of bureaucratic hyper-rationalism" (10) represented there. Each slide in the presentation, according to Tufte, con-tains "4 to 6 levels of hierarchy," provides no continuity from slide to slide, and ultimately serves to complicate and obscure what are already difficult technical issues. Eventually, Tufte cites the Columbia Accident Investigation Board's report in support of his own conclusions "that the distinctive cognitive style of PowerPoint reinforced the hierarchical filtering and biases of the NASA bureaucracy during the crucial period when the Columbia was damaged but still functioning" (12). It would perhaps be a stretch to blame the Columbia disaster on PowerPoint, but, as Tufte makes clear, not much of one. "The language, attitude, and presentation tool of the pitch culture had penetrated throughout the NASA organization, even into the most serious technical analysis, the survival of the shuttle" (12). Whether or not we want to go so far as to blame the presentation tool, Tufte is clear that PowerPoint had a marked effect on the communications of the organization and fatal consequences for the crew of the Columbia. Tufte's claims circulated well beyond the traditional audience for such analysis; his condemnation of PowerPoint was not only covered by *Wired* but by Sunday's *New York Times Magazine* under the headline "PowerPoint Makes You Dumb." Tufte's essay has also appeared in countless classrooms, an archetypal critique of the problems of uncritically adopting and using software.

As a result of his critique's ubiquity, if there is one person who has done more to shape the academy's attitude towards slideware, it is probably Tufte. But it is worth considering in more detail the perspective compositionists have endorsed. In one sense, Tufte is an obvious ally for writing teachers; as he explains, "Serious problems require a serious tool: written reports" (14). Although an abbreviated form of Tufte's essay appeared in *Wired* with the headline "PowerPoint is Evil," his broader argument is not that PowerPoint is essentially wrong, but rather that print writing is more important than we sometimes imagine. In the case of Columbia, information was circulating, as well as decisions made that were based upon that information, in a form inappropriate to the detail and sophistication needed. The second major argument that Tufte offers in his essay has to do with information density and PowerPoint users' tendency to compromise density in favor of readable font sizes, copious negative space, and meaningless clip art. Given the criterion of information density, Tufte finds PowerPoint wanting on almost every level. The "simple tables" permitted by slides are compared with John Graunt's 1662 "Table of Causalities," which, as Tufte explains, would have required 155 slides to present what Graunt accomplishes in a single page. Standard injunctions about the number of bullet points per slide and words per line reduce potentially complex topics to the diction of first-grade reading primers. In short, Tufte explains, "The PP slide format has the worst signal/noise ratio of any known method of communication on paper or computer screen" (26). As a discipline devoted, in many ways, to the "signal," it is unsurprising that we would find these arguments persuasive.

There have been a few challenges to Tufte's conclusions, however, worth considering; one such appeared from Donald Norman, whose work on design qualifies him easily as a peer of Tufte's. In a 2004 interview with Cliff Atkinson, Norman lays out the ideas that would later turn into an essay, "In

Defense of PowerPoint," published at his own website. In that essay, Norman describes Tufte's conclusions as "nonsense;" he argues that the NASA slides, however poorly executed, reflected similarly mistaken findings on the part of the engineers. "The fault is with the findings, not with the slides . . . they highlighted the information they thought important and minimized the parts they thought not important. That is the absolutely proper way to present a set of recommendations" ("In Defense"). Norman's broader point is that information density is a standard more appropriate to the reader than the listener, and that "the speech giver should really develop three different documents:" personal notes, slides, and handouts, each designed to meet different goals as part of a presentation. From a disciplinary perspective, Norman qualifies Tufte's argument in an important way: information density is not a context-independent value. This doesn't necessarily invalidate Tufte's critique, nor does it absolve poor presentations of any responsibility. But it should prompt us to think about those contexts where PowerPoint might actually be appropriate and, used well, a platform that can enrich the role of design and delivery in our writing pedagogies. As design takes a more central place in composition pedagogy, the PowerPoint renaissance that has occurred in the business and design world in recent years challenges us to consider the role of slideware more seriously.

Matters of Slideware Design

As evident in a growing number of articles and textbooks in our field, design has a growing influence in composition pedagogy; Richard Marback refers to it in a recent issue of *College Composition and Communication* as a "centripetal interest" for our discipline (398). In a 2001 *Philosophy and Rhetoric* article, Richard Buchanan suggests we can think of design as "the human power of conceiving, planning, and making products that serve human beings in the accomplishment of any individual or collective purpose" (qtd. in "Design" 191). To think of design, then, as "styling of appearance of products," Buchanan argues, is a serious misconception of what the work of designing entails (194). Like rhetoric, design is an art of forethought, whose work occurs deeply in the act of invention, arrangement, and production. Design, like rhetoric, is a productive act of making.

Anne Wysocki and Dennis Lynch's handbook, *Compose, Design, Advocate,* is perhaps the most explicit in articulating the important function of design can play in the writing classroom. While acknowledging that the discipline of composition has always been closely linked with rhetoric, Wysocki and Lynch point out that because of changes in communication technologies, particularly the digital, thinking about design has become especially pertinent. As Wysocki and Lynch point out, the fields of composition and rhetoric and design share similar concerns—"both are concerned with audiences and with how audiences respond to what we make" (5). Yet, design also differs from composition and rhetoric in that design is more concerned with: a) the material and creative process of composing; b) testing the audience's experiences with the products; and c) the future functions of the product once it enters into circulation. Such concerns, Wysocki and Lynch note, have the potential to enhance our students' composing processes as they learn to anticipate and consider the responses their artifacts might invoke in the daily lives of their audience.

Students also, and perhaps most importantly, learn to consider which different media are most appropriate to use in achieving their rhetorical goals. Because PowerPoint has gotten a "bad rap" in recent years from figures such as Tufte, the innovative and rhetorical potential of slideware is often overlooked. Contemporary designers, however, make a strong case as to why slideware presentations should take a more important role in the writing classroom. The design of slideware cannot only enhance our students' abilities to think creatively about problems that matter, but also to communicate clearly in designs that matter. In addition, slideware design makes use of whole- mind aptitudes, which many argue are needed to communicate successfully and persuasively in today's global arena.

Nancy Duarte's book *slide:ology: The Art and Science of Generating Great Presentations* is one text that makes a strong case for thinking about slideware as an innovative writing technology that can boost our students' creative thinking. Duarte—the designer behind *An Inconvenient Truth*—situates PowerPoint at the tail end of a long history of visual storytelling that begins nearly 2,000 years ago with the oldest cave painting found to date in Lascaux, France. Duarte rejects Tufte's argument that PowerPoint reduces the analytical quality of presentations and weakens verbal and spatial reasoning. Instead, she suggests that PowerPoint can be a productive visual aid for generating innovative ideas and communicating creatively, clearly, and effectively for a given audience. As evidence, in *slide:ology* Duarte illustrates how PowerPoint design is revitalizing the role of multimedia presentations in the business world. Case studies are woven throughout her text to illustrate how creative PowerPoint presentations are not only saving business people from committing "career suislide," but also enhancing the production and reception of presentations performed by today's most innovative thinkers. At intellectual gatherings such as the highly prestigious TED and PopTech conferences, the innovative role of slideware is certainly pervasive, giving rise, in many people's opinion, to some of the most compelling media presentations ever produced.

In *slide:ology* Duarte offers composition teachers and students a useful framework for thinking about the development process of slideware as a "presentation ecosystem" constituted by an interdependence of innovative ideas, effective (rhetorical, in essence) delivery, and visual design (11). Too often, visual design in composition classrooms is simply thought of as an act and sign of "academic decorum" (George 25). Students, in other words, use visual design to demonstrate their attention to document design. In slideware, this act translates to mere concern with representation. *slide:ology* demonstrates how visual design is actually a highly conceptual and creative communicative act that can help students solve problems by generating new ideas. For instance, by sketching ideas and creating diagrams to communicate abstract ideas in their slide presentations, students can find relationships between information that leads to new insights and generates deeper understanding between audience and presenter. In *slide:ology* the creative process of designing slides is positioned, in other words, as not simply the representation of ideas but rather the generation of ideas. In this sense, slideware becomes an important means of invention, dispelling notions of slideware simply as a means of delivery.

Garr Reynolds's book *Presentation Zen,* in conjunction with its active accompanying website, also offers composition teachers and students a fresh outlook on the productive possibilities afforded by slideware design. Garr Reynolds is a leading consultant in presentation design and delivery for Fortune 500 companies around the globe. He conceived the idea for this book after growing frustrated by the ubiquity of poorly designed and difficult-to-understand presentations riddled with bullet points, crammed text, and egregious clip art. Reynolds calls such poorly and thoughtlessly designed slide presentations "slideuments," which he claims are created more from a desire to save time rather than generate effective presentations. Reynolds argues that PowerPoint as a tool is not to blame, however. If used to create simple, balanced, and beautiful designs in conjunction with a well-crafted story and delivery style, PowerPoint presentations can be highly effective in achieving one's communicative goal(s). Unlike the conventional demonizations of PowerPoint by Parker, Tufte, and others, Reynolds argues and illustrates that PowerPoint is a tool capable of creating intelligent, emotional, and effective communication.

Reynolds's book offers students an "approach" to slideware rather than a method, one that relies heavily on Zen principles[2] relating to aesthetics, mindfulness, and connectedness. As Reynolds explains, a method of presentation design and delivery might offer a set of design rules to be adhered to by everyone in the same way. In contrast, the philosophical approach of *presentationzen* emphasizes a flexible path to designing and delivering presentations that encourage audience awareness, creativity, and discovery (25). Reynolds's main argument can be essentially wrapped up in one line: *Design Matters to Clear Communication.* Reiterating Duarte's argument that design is not about decoration or ornamentation, Reynolds emphasizes that design is, to a great extent, about making communication as easy and clear as possible for one's viewers (163). Thus, design matters because audience matters—a lesson we cannot impress enough upon our students in the composition classroom. To achieve simple, clear, and effective communication, Reynolds suggests being constantly mindful of the principles of restraint, simplicity, and naturalness: "Restraint in preparation. Simplicity in design. Naturalness in delivery" (7). Such mindfulness, he argues, has the potential to generate innovative and effective communication, especially if it becomes a permanent way of thinking about design and delivery.

The design values embodied in both Reynolds's and Duarte's ideas on presentation and delivery are aligned with contemporary notions about the role of creative thinking and design in effective persuasion. While writing instructors might not typically look to contemporary arguments made about communication offered in best selling business books, such arguments challenge us in productive ways to rethink the relation between slideware design and persuasion. Reynolds's approach, for instance, draws deeply on Daniel Pink's right-brain aptitudes as discussed in *A Whole New Mind.* In composition and rhetoric classrooms, analytical thinking is often the privileged form of knowing that we teach in relation to rhetoric and argument. Pink would argue that such logical, linear, and analytical, or left-brain thinking, skills are no longer sufficient to prepare students to communicate effectively in the "Conceptual Age" in which we presently find ourselves. According to Pink, students need to develop "high concept" aptitudes, which include detecting patterns and opportunities, generating creative and emotional beauty, crafting appealing narratives, and synthesizing unrelated ideas to generate new ones (2). Pink especially emphasizes that it is not enough to make logical arguments in order to persuade. We need to be able to create compelling narratives, which Pink argues is at the heart of effective persuasion. In addition, while analysis is obviously still necessary, the ability to empathize and synthesize, see the big picture, and identify interconnectivity is increasingly becoming important to successful global communication. From a design perspective, these abilities, which are fostered through slideware design, are needed to communicate effectively and create effective presentations in today's professional world.

Arguments about the importance of design to persuasion are also evident in Chip Heath and Dan Heath's principles for communicating ideas that stick. In their book, *Made to Stick,* Heath and Heath argue that "sticky" ideas have six common principles: simplicity, unexpectedness, concreteness, credibility, emotions, and stories. Too often, Heath and Heath argue, presenters suffer from what they call the "Curse of Knowledge"—the condition whereby the deliverer overestimates an audience's background knowledge about the topic at hand. Presenters who suffer this condition often create abstract claims that are perfectly clear to the presenter, but barely, if at all, comprehendible to the audience. Scholars who attend highly theoretical conference presentations in our own field will recognize this curse. Too often conference presentations couched in dense theories and discourse fail to make an impact on an audience, not because their ideas are not smart and important, but simply because the language is too abstract for an audience to absorb in a 20-minute session falling in the midst of a long day of conference-going. Their ideas simply are too abstract to stick. Heath and Heath offer a counterargument to Tufte's claim that PowerPoint has too poor of a signal/noise ratio to be effective or appropriate by arguing for the value of a low signal/noise ratio in slideware presentations. While Tufte would argue slideware lacks the ability to convey complex ideas needed in specific rhetorical situations, Heath and Heath—alongside Reynolds and Duarte—argue that simplifying a message actually amplifies the clarity and effect of a complex message. Heath and Heath suggest avoiding too many statistics or, in our field, too many dense quotes, which often stem from over-attempts to establish one's credibility. In addition, Heath and Heath advocate for surprising the audience and speaking of concrete images to increase the stickiness of a message. Making some kind of emotional connections with our audiences and incorporating an element of story in our presentations are also effective ways to create persuasive messages that audience members will remember.

While such principles for effective communication and persuasion, offered by experts in the design and business worlds, may not seem profound or even new to scholars of rhetoric and composition, these applied principles encourage us to rethink the value of slideware design in our classrooms. Unlike Parker, Tufte, and others who see little value in PowerPoint's ability to generate and deliver innovative ideas, design professionals such as Duarte and Reynolds argue and illustrate that we ought to take slideware more seriously as a creative and intelligent tool. First, integrating slideware into our pedagogy has the potential to enhance certain aptitudes and design perspectives that can make students more effective communicators. Second, if taught as a process, slideware can help bridge verbal, visual, and oral communication skills, which still so often get divorced in much writing pedagogy. Also, in addition to improving our students' chances to make their ideas stick, slideware presentation, as we aim to illustrate in the next section, can especially help students realize and make use of design's inventive affordances. For these reasons, we argue it is time that writing teachers take slideware more seriously in our writing classrooms.

Slideware in the Classroom

Integrating slideware successfully and meaningfully into our classrooms depends on rethinking the role and location of delivery in the composing process and reconsidering the productivity of constraint writing, presentation design, and visual thinking. In rethinking the role of delivery, James Porter and others argue that we need to think about how delivery connects to productive, inventional thinking rather than simply a means to disseminate information. For many of us, such reconfiguration of delivery works against all that we have been taught about the composing process. As Kathleen Yancey notes in her recently published NCTE report *Writing in the 21st Century*, in print-based models of composing, delivery has long been associated with publication or presentation—the final stage of the writing process. The writing process, of course, has been taught as recursive; we all know that invention, style, revision, and arrangement do not happen in chronological order. However, in terms of recursivity, at least in many of our classrooms, delivery by and large has been, and still is, conceived and taught as the final act of the composing process—or in more ecological terms, the final stage in the life cycle of a text. As the final stage, the role of delivery is simply to translate one's print-based arguments into oral, visual, or multi-media form and to present one's final arguments to a broader audience. As such, in writing instruction, John Trimbur argues, "delivery has been an afterthought at best, assigned mainly to technical and professional communication and associated largely with such matters of document design as page layout, typography, visual display of information, and Web design ("Composition" 190). Delivery, in other words, is a "technical issue about physical presentation" rather than a practice of invention (190). It is the final touch we put on our already completed written ideas, one that has little to do with the ideas themselves.

A visualization of presentation or delivery being the "last act" cannot be more palpable than in Ruth Culham and Vicki Spandel's 6 + 1 Trait framework. This model is billed as an assessment method, but it is currently being used all over the nation as a writing instruction method for secondary English education. According to this model, presentation is the "+1," added onto and othered from the list of more core traits of idea development and organization. In addition, presentation is positioned outside the recursive process, which only encompasses pre-writing, drafting, responding, and revision. Such frameworks are reinforced in our college composition classrooms when we assign PowerPoints as the culminating assignment in our curricula—when we ask students to visually and orally express their ideas that they have already thought through, polished, and presented in formal writing assignments.

This truncation of delivery as a final, almost inessential, stage in the composing process positions it as exterior to invention. In Derridean terms, delivery conceived here is a supplement, both in that the role of delivery is created by its opposition to invention and that is it is often seen as an unsuitable substitute for invention. As supplement, delivery cannot be trusted as a core trait (if we want to use that term), nor can it be "trusted" as a productive stage in the composing process with the potential to help students develop creative and analytical thought. Continuing to conceive of and to teach delivery according to traditional print-based models of composing necessarily limits the role that slideware might play in the composing process. Using the presentation format Pecha Kucha as a model, we aim to illustrate how slideware can provide writers with meaningful acts of rhetorical transformation, especially when we permit invention to be constituted by delivery, resituating it to a more productive place in our writing curricula.

Pecha Kucha is a contemporary form of presentation design and delivery[3] revitalizing the role of PowerPoint in the design world. The method of Pecha Kucha entails telling a story in sync with 20 slides, shown for 20 seconds each. As Daniel Pink has described the format, "That's it. Say what you need to say in six minutes and 40 seconds and then sit the hell down." Pecha Kucha derives from the Japanese term for "the sound of conversation" or "chit-chat." As originally conceived by Astrid Klein and Mark Dytham, this presentation format affords designers a brief, but potent, means to share their work in public spaces with other designers. In other words, Pecha Kucha began as a designer's adult version of "show and tell." Since its inception in Tokyo in 2003, Pecha Kucha nights have become a global phenomenon in which professionals from the design, architecture, photography, and other creative fields meet, network, and present their current work in public venues.

In the writing classroom, the Pecha Kucha format has transformative affordances that emerge when slideware is used to construct arguments rather than present *already* composed, written arguments. To a great extent, these features emerge when we ask students to work with format and design constraints. In *The Laws of Simplicity,* John Maeda explains, "In the design world, there is the belief that with more constraints, better solutions are revealed" (qtd. in Reynolds 39). Extending this point, Reynolds also argues, "[C]onstraints and limitations are a powerful ally, not an enemy" (39). Working within constraints with the trust that restrictions can be liberators, Reynolds claims, creates clear and powerful messages (39). In the composition classroom, constrained writing has been under-appreciated. As Jan Baetens explains, we can think of constrained writing as "the use of any type of formal technique or program whose application is able to produce a sense of its making text by itself, if need be without any previous "idea" from the writer" ("Freewriting" 2). A constraint-ruled text is opposed to a text in which an author attempts to articulate an idea that was realized before he or she sits down to write (2). Typically, in the composition classroom, we associate constrained writing with a current-traditionalist approach and thus neglect to explore how constraints can be an important part of the inventive process. Yet, as Baetens make clear, constraints can act as a meaningful imaginative tool if an integrated relationship is created between constraints and the entire production process.

Baetens distinguishes between dissociative and integrative processes of constrained writing. Dissociative approaches ask students to work with one constraint in the production of a text. When constructing a Pecha Kucha, for instance, a dissociative approach would impose one rule students must abide by, such as using two sentences per slide and in conjunction with one image. Working within the confines of a single contrived constraint, students are able to dissociate from the design process to a certain degree. An integrative approach, on the other hand, asks students to work with permanent constraints throughout the whole production of their Pecha Kuchas. Unlike a dissociative model, in an integrative process, constraints have the potential to mutually shape all parameters of the work (Baetens). An integrative approach to creating Pecha Kuchas is encouraged when we ask students to abide by presentation design principles forwarded by Reynolds to tell the story of their 10-12 page first-draft, researched arguments in 6 minute and 40 second Pecha Kuchas. Design constraints are conceived as aesthetic values, rather than rules, to be considered through every step of the production process. For example, students are asked to strive for simplicity, balance, subtlety, elegance, naturalness, and tranquility. These values are achieved by using empty space, relevant elements or information, clear and simple display of information, 2-D rather than 3-D representations, repetition of visual elements, contrast, alignment, etc. These design principles, offered by both Reynolds and Duarte, place constraints on slide design throughout the entire production of Pecha Kuchas. In terms of the oral part of their presentation, students are encouraged to avoid reading from a script, move from behind the podium, keep the lights on, and attempt to make some kind of emotional connection with the audience. While these constraints often intimidate students, we also have begun to observe many students taking risks and generating dynamic presentations. Thus, rather than act as creative obstacles, such integrated interaction with constraints stimulates visual play and innovative presentation design.

Constraints, although difficult to work with, help students create visual presentations that are rhetorically powerful. When positioned as rhetorical strategies, students' design choices help them achieve their communicative goals. Yet even more importantly, the integrated process of working with constraints is transformative, especially when we relocate delivery to the middle of our students composing process. In our critical research and writing courses[4], for instance, students begin by crafting full drafts of a written argument. Students then research for, design, and craft their Pecha Kuchas with the goal of narrating the exigency for their study, their findings, and their current arguments about the topic at hand. Students present their ideas in a Pecha Kucha to the class during a Pecha Kucha Night event. After they present their Pecha Kuchas, and the class discusses them, we ask the students to go back to the page to reconstruct their arguments in light of that discussion. Integrating the design and presentation of Pecha Kuchas *into* the composing process helps students revise their initial print-based arguments, not only in terms of organization but also in the development of ideas. The 20 x 20 slideware format obliges students to identify and emphasize only the most relevant ideas in their longer arguments. In rewriting their final print documents, students often omit material included in their original print arguments when they realize it was not significant enough to include in their Pecha Kuchas. At the same time, students often end up rearranging their final written essays to create a more coherent argument. Constructing Pecha Kuchas helps students understand how their written arguments could be more effectively arranged on the page. As a result of deploying slideware *during* the composing process, rather than as an afterthought, students craft powerful narratives that end up resulting in tighter and sharper arguments on the page.

When finding visuals to include in their Pecha Kuchas, students also often discover new information that extends, complicates, and contradicts their previous arguments. Some students even realize that the original focus of their previous arguments is no longer the main point they want to or need to be focusing on. Students develop new ideas, in other words, by working through the composing process of creating their Pecha Kuchas. In an interview with Nancy Duarte about her work with Al Gore, Duarte explains that Gore was "constantly learning from each presentation and refining his message and his visuals along the way" ("Duarte Design"). Similarly, Pecha Kucha stimulates rhetorical revision of students' initial arguments. The rhetorical revision that slideware can provoke has important inventive implications. Our teaching experience similarly indicates that students often have a difficult time "re-seeing" their work and realizing that much of the revision process is actually an act of letting go and developing new directions for their work. They have a difficult idea time buying into the notion, in other words, that revision is constituted by invention just as invention is constituted by delivery. Asking students to switch modalities in the midst of their composing process to design a multimedia presentation of their argument engages them fully in this process, however. Resituating "presentation" in the composing process can help students work recursively between visual and print, as well as other interactive stages of the 21st century composing process. In effect, through the design and production of slideware, students realize inventive possibilities in their own work that the invisibility of typical print- based writing may not encourage.

It is important to note here that the transformative possibilities afforded by slideware exist only when we take time to teach slideware as a presentation design process, which entails crafting a message, designing a visual story, and thinking through delivery. In teaching slideware, the instructor must do more than simply show students how to operate the software. If our pedagogical focus rests solely on the technical—the mastery of the software's basic features—then much of the potential of slideware will be unavailable to us. Following Reynolds, Duarte, and others, slideware can provide us with an opportunity to teach presentation as a sensitive ecosystem, balanced by attention to content, design, and delivery. In our classes, we devote nearly six weeks or one unit to discuss and implement the innovative design and delivery principles offered in *Presentation Zen* and *slide:ology*. During this unit, the classroom is turned into a studio environment where students are creating storyboards, crafting narrative, using visual search engines, playing with Photoshop, designing visuals, creating handouts, and practicing delivery. Rather than being an afterthought, then, slideware is positioned as a rhetorical strategy and a productive means of invention, persuasion, and revision.

We also find that when we ask students to engage in presentation design, many engage in visual thinking, which often triggers creative potentials not accessed in print-based composition. Visual thinking is as highly unstable in meaning as rhetoric itself. Yet, for our purposes, as Dawan Stanford helps us understand, visual thinking, most broadly, can be thought of as "the use and exploration of images as tools for communication, understanding, creativity, problem solving, and explanation" ("What is"). Visual thinking[5] entails such activities as making and using sketches, diagrams, and graphs to think through abstract concepts, generate ideas, make decisions, problem solve and/or illustrate relations between information. Other activities, among many, include creating tag clouds, concept mapping, and data visualization. Visual thinking, as conceived here, is different than visual rhetorics. As articulated in *Defining Visual Rhetorics,* visual rhetorics, in a broad sense, is most often thought of in two ways: as an artifact that individuals create for communicative purposes and as a perspective or lens employed to study how visual artifacts perform rhetorically (303). Visual rhetorics, we would argue, is just one realm of visual thinking. While visual rhetorics is receiving growing attention in composition studies, visual thinking, in its creative, explanatory, and problem-solving sense, has received little attention in composition and rhetoric.

Our work with slideware in the classroom suggests that many of our students, especially those majoring in the design arts, benefit from stimulating visual thinking to generate productive reasoning, creativity, and communicative fluency. Visual thinking can trigger non-linear, intuitive, and creative thought processes that often, in turn, unlock modes of thought not accessed via linear, logical thought processes (see Rudolf Arnheim's classic text *Visual Thinking*). When students engage in presentation design and visual thinking during the construction of presentations, students are able to access this creative mode of thought that helps to generate new ways of thinking about their topics. This ability to switch between logical and creative modes of thought, in turn, enhances our students' potential to employ their whole mind to generate compelling arguments. As Eva Brumberger argues, visual thinking is important for helping students move fluidly between and within different modes of thought and communication ("Making," 378). When we prepare students to think verbally, but not visually, Brumberger argues, we "risk producing writers who are visual technicians—writers skilled in visual tools and techniques but lacking what Hocks and Kendrick (2003) referred to such ability as 'fully hybrid eloquence'" (378). Such eloquence entails thinking of visual and verbal modes of communication as complementary and being able to move fluently and creatively back and forth between the two to achieve one's communicative and problem-solving goals. Students training to be professional and technical writers especially need to develop ambidexterity in terms of thought and communication style to succeed in the workplace (Brumberger 2007; Johnson-Sheehan, 2002; Olsen, 1991; Stroupe, 2000). As our field takes on the responsibility to prepare technical and professional writers, we argue that when taught as a presentation development process, PowerPoint offers student opportunities to hone this ability.

At least one other significant affordance also emerges. As the creators of Pecha Kucha explain, "Pecha Kucha is a *real* social network" in which presenters interact with each other's ideas throughout the evening in a casual atmosphere (Dytham and Klein 18). In the composition classroom, because of the typical ways in which we position delivery, students too often think of presentations as formal, final reports of their work rather than opportunities to stimulate casual conversation about their ideas. Assimilating Pecha Kucha events in our classrooms, however, repositions delivery as occasions to share their ideas and learn from peer and instructor responses, especially if we omit the typical, stifled Q & A sessions in favor of opportunities for students to casually discuss each other's work. In post-Pecha Kucha reflections, students claim that their peers' presentations and the subsequent conversations actually provoke new ideas about their own arguments. In effect, students' final written arguments become utterances in Bahktinian terms—responses to and determined by previous utterances. If repositioned in *media res* of the composing process, slideware design and delivery helps students begin to see that their writing can generate a response from an intended viewer. This response may or may not be the one they hoped to evoke; yet, no matter—by hearing the responses and seeing how their own work stimulates dialogue, they come to see how their final compositions act as *utterances* generated as part of and for the purpose of dialogue. A tighter social network of writers, rhetors, and designers is thus created in the classroom community. Students begin to take their own as well as their peers' ideas more seriously.

Conclusion

Despite the universal disdain we hold in writing studies for the five-paragraph theme, no one would suggest that we do without paragraphs themselves in our writing, and yet, this is the curious position that most slideware occupies for us. PowerPoint, Keynote, and the rest are judged by the very worst examples of what they can accomplish, leading us to resist their use in our classrooms. This in turn often means that we spend little time exploring or negotiating the software, either on our own or with our students, and this results in the very types of presentation that we dread. Our failure to take slideware seriously as a writing platform keeps us trapped in a vicious circle, one marked by mediocre presentations and an unwillingness to engage seriously the very tools that might help us improve them. We argue for a pedagogical renaissance of slideware in the writing classroom; coupled with contemporary design theories, slideware has the potential to revitalize student writing at all stages of the composing process. Slideware repositions our students as makers and designers in addition to writers and rhetors.

In the *Nicomachean Ethics*, Aristotle distinguishes among the modalities of knowing, doing, and making, suggesting that each has its own values and criteria by which we measure them. One of the striking things about rhetoric and writing, as well as design, is that they cut across all three. While the earliest days of the process movement attested to our ability to know through writing, and the social turn of the past twenty years has emphasized symbolic action and writing as a form of doing, our recent disciplinary forays into multimedia and networked writing encourage us to recover the third term, *making*, as well. It is not ultimately a matter of choosing one over the others, but rather, critically integrating them in a way that allows all three to inform each other. We would not necessarily suggest that slideware presentations supplant more traditional academic essays, but we have found that, as an element of the process rather than an afterthought, slideware can encourage our students to attend more closely to the ways that they *make* as they write. This sense of design can productively complicate their work, make them more conscious of their choices, and help them to develop a better sense of their own rhetorical effectiveness.

Notes

1. Although for many years, PowerPoint has been synonymous with what we call "slideware," a wide array of applications exists that permit the sequential display of slides. For this reason, in this essay, while we center much of the discussion around PowerPoint, we prefer the broader designation of "slideware."

2. Some scholars may certainly scowl at Reynolds' appropriation of Zen imagery and philosophical principles for slideware design and criticize his explanation of Zen for its reductive qualities. Yet, from an affirmative perspective, the "Presentation Zen approach" does offer a straightforward and, we would argue innovative, way to reconceptualize the value of PowerPoint.
3. Inspired by Pecha Kuchas, Ignite is a similar presentation genre in which presenters show 20 slides that automatically rotate after 15 seconds, creating a 5-minute presentation. Started in Seattle in 2006 by Brady Forrest and Bre Pettis, Ignite has two parts: an Ignite contest and Ignite talks. Community members can decide on what contest they want to hold and then recruit speakers to present.
4. The Pecha Kucha assignment as discussed in this article has been implemented in several sections of WRT 205 at Syracuse University. WRT 205 is a required critical research and writing course designed to be taken during students' sophomore year. The claims made about the value of resituating presentation and the value of constrained writing in the composing process are based on student reflections, teacher observations, and one-on-one conversations with students. No formal study of this assignment has been conducted. This article grows out of the authors' interest in pedagogical exploration of slideware and delivery in the writing classroom, rather than a report of research findings.
5. For an excellent discussion of visual thinking in relation to communication, see Brumberger.

Works Cited

Aristotle. *Nicomachean Ethics*. Trans. and Ed. Roger Crisp. Cambridge: Cambridge UP, 2000. Print.

Arnheim, Rudolf. *Visual Thinking*. Berkeley: U of California P, 1972. Print.

Atkinson, Cliff. "PowerPoint Usability: Q&A with Don Norman." *Socialmedia*. (2004): n. pag. Web. 10 Oct. 2009.

Baetens, Jan. "Comic Strips and Constrained Writing." *Image [&] Narrative*. Oct (2003): n. pag. Web. 15 Oct. 2009.

———. "Free Writing, Constrained Writing: The Ideology of Form." *Poetics Today*. 18.1 (1997): 1-14. Print.

Brumberger, Eva R. "Making the Strange Familiar: A Pedagogical Exploration of Visual Thinking." *Journal of Business and Technical Communication*. 21 (2007): 376-401. Print.

Buchanan, Richard. "Design and the New Rhetoric: Productive Arts in the Philosophy of Culture." *Philosophy and Rhetoric*. 34.3 (2001): 183-206. Print.

Duarte, Nancy. *slide:ology: The Art and Science of Creating Great Presentations*. Cambridge: O'Reilly Media, Inc., 2008. Print.

Dytham, Mark, and Astrid Klein. *Pecha Kucha Night: 20 Images x 20 Seconds*. Tokyo: Klein Dytham, 2008. Print.

Heath, Chip, and Dan Heath. *Made to Stick: Why Some Ideas Survive and Others Die*. New York: Random House, 2007. Print.

George, Diana. "From Analysis to Design: Visual Communication in the Teaching of Writing." *College Composition and Communication.* 52.1 (September 2002): 11-39. Print.

Johnson-Sheehan, R. "Being Visual, Visual Beings." In *Working with Words and Images: New Steps in an Old Dance.* Ed. Allen.. Westport, CT: Ablex, 2002. Print.

Maeda, John. *The Laws of Simplicity (Simplicity: Design, Technology, Business, Life).* Cambridge: MIT P, 2006. Print.

Marback, Richard. "Embracing Wicked Problems: The Turn to Design in Composition Studies." *College Composition and Communication* 61.2 (2009): 397-419. Print.

Norman, Donald. "In Defense of PowerPoint." *jnd.org.* 2004. Web. 10 Oct. 2009.

Olsen, G. R. "Eidetecker: The Professional Communicator in the New Visual Culture." *IEEE Transactions on Professional Communication.* 34 (1991): 13-19. Print.

Pink, Daniel. *A Whole New Mind: Why Right-Brainers Will Rule the Future.* New York: Riverhead Books, 2005. Print.

Parker, Ian. "Absolute PowerPoint: Can a Software Package Edit our Thoughts?" *The New Yorker* 77.13 (2001): 76–87. Print.

Porter, James E.. "Recovering Delivery for Digital Rhetoric and Human-Computer Interaction." 2 Feb 2010. Web.

Reynolds, Garr. *Presentation Zen: Simple Ideas on Presentation Design and Delivery.* Berkeley: New Riders, 2008. Print.

———. "Duarte Design Helps Al Gore "go visual." *Presentation Zen Blog.* 01 June 2006. Web. 10 Oct. 2009.

Stanford, Dawan. "What is Visual Thinking? (definition 1.0)" *Fluidhive Blog.* 8 June 2009. Web. 2 Feb. 2010.

Stroupe, C. "Visualizing English: Recognizing the Hybrid Literacy of Visual and Verbal Authorship on the Web." *College English* 62 (2000): 607-32. Print.

Trimbur, John. "Composition and the Circulation of Writing." *College Composition and Communication* 52.2. (2000): 188–219.

Tufte, Edward. "The Cognitive Style of PowerPoint: Pitching Out Corrupts Within." *The Work of Edward Tufte and Graphics Press.* 6 Sep 2005. Web. 10 October 2009.

———. "PowerPoint is Evil: Power Corrupts. PowerPoint Corrupts Absolutely." *Wired* 11.09 (September 2003): n. pag. Web. 10 Oct. 2009.

Yancey, Kathleen. "Writing in the 21st Century: A Report from the National Council of Teachers of English." Urbana: *NCTE.org.* 2009. Web. 10 Oct. 2009.

The Genre Effect: Exploring the Unfamiliar

Heather Bastian

Much composition pedagogy begins writing instruction within familiar territory. As a result, composition educators often structure curriculum and courses so that students first write in familiar genres, like personal narratives, and examine and critique their own lives, experiences, and even beliefs through those genres before turning to unfamiliar territory. Many compositionists also use that familiar territory to foster and develop students' critical consciousness, defined by Paulo Freire in his influential *Pedagogy of the Oppressed* as "learning to perceive social, political, and economic contradictions and to take action against the oppressive elements of reality" (35). Composition educators, of course, want to help students develop their writing skills and abilities, but in doing so many also invite students to uncover, critique, and resist underlying ideological dimensions present in the discourses of their everyday lives through the critical examination of the familiar.

One impetus for beginning within the familiar can be found within Lev Vygotsky's "zone of proximal development," which he defines as "the distance between the actual developmental level as determined by independent problem solving and the level of potential development as determined through problem solving under adult guidance, or in collaboration with more capable peers" (86). Vygostky, and many others after him, suggests that teachers provide students with experiences that are within their zone of proximal development in order to encourage learning. Another impetus can be found within the works of John Dewey, in which he argues that educators must connect student interests to the material and classroom. For example, in *Interest and Effort in Education,* he suggests that to "make things interesting," subjects should "be selected in relation to the child's present experience, powers, and needs; and that . . . the new material be presented in such a way to enable the child to appreciate its bearings, its relationships, and its value in connection with what already has significance for him" (23-24). And yet another impetus can be found in the wide-scale admonishment of the "banking concept of education" and the adoption of various kinds of "problem-posing education" (Freire, Shor). An integral component of "problem-posing education" is, as Ira Shor suggests, to "situate learning in the students' cultures—their literacy, their themes, their present cognitive and affective levels, their aspiration, their daily lives" (24). Certainly these theoretical foundations and arguments are not only reasonable, but valuable, and have lead to many productive uses of the familiar within the writing classroom. However, as with all pedagogical approaches, there are some limitations to beginning with the familiar, especially when one of the goals of the composition classroom is to develop critical consciousness.

In this essay, I consider some of the problems students and teachers may encounter when beginning within familiar territory and then provide yet another option for how a composition course might begin writing instruction to foster students' critical consciousness. To do so, I examine how one pedagogical approach, the explicit teaching of genre, incorporates the familiar, mainly through familiar genres, and then I explore the difficulties that students may encounter when beginning within familiar genres. I argue that these difficulties may lie within our own assumptions about composition pedagogy and critical consciousness as well as the ideological forces of genres and what I am terming as the *genre effect*. From this, I expand upon current approaches to the explicit teaching of genre by proposing and exploring a pedagogy that considers the *genre effect* and invites students to begin not with the familiar but with the unfamiliar.

The Explicit Teaching of Genre and the Familiar

The explicit teaching of genre differs from other approaches to writing instruction in that it understands genres as "typified rhetorical actions based in recurrent situations" (Miller 31). Genres, in this light, are not just forms or rules to follow; instead, as Charles Bazerman writes, "Genres are forms of life, ways of being. They are frames for social action. They are environments for learning. They are locations within which meaning is constructed. Genres shape the thoughts we form and the communications by which we interact" ("Life" 19). With this understanding, everyday texts like cereal boxes, horoscopes, and billboards are considered worthy of study as genres, in addition to traditionally identified genres such as novels, poems, research papers, personal narratives, movies, etc.

Genres, however, are not simply actions occurring within a void—they are actions based within specific, social, and recurrent rhetorical situations, thus making genre rhetorical in nature. As such, the explicit teaching of genre is grounded within analysis of not only genre but also the rhetorical situations (participants, subject[s], purpose[s], and setting[s]) in which genres are located since, as Amy Devitt writes, "genre and situation are tightly interwoven . . . it is genre that determines situation as well as situation that determines genre" (23). In other words, the relationship between genre and rhetorical situation is reciprocal, so the two are interrelated—one can look to a genre to understand elements of the rhetorical situation and one can look to the rhetorical situation to understand elements of the genre.

If genres are social actions based in recurrent rhetorical situations, then they also contain ideological components that structure and influence users' perceptions of the world and actions (Schyrer, Devitt). Devitt explains that "because people in groups develop genres, genres reflect what the group believes and how it views the world" (59). Genres represent and reinforce what participants within certain rhetorical situations value, believe, and assume. For example, many engaged heterosexual couples within the United States create wedding invitations that employ certain rhetorical choices and moves (such as "Mr. and Mrs. John Smith request the honor of your presence at the marriage of their daughter Ann Smith to David Jones") that reflect culturally prescribed and valued gender norms and promote heterosexual unions and cultures. If genres are understood as social actions with embedded ideological commitments that are grounded within rhetorical situations, then genres become ideal sites for students to develop a critical consciousness of the ways in which ideologies act on and through people.

Scholars such as Anis Bawarshi, Charles Bazerman, Robert Brooke and Dale Jacobs, Kevin Brooks, Richard Coe, Amy Devitt, Lorelei Lingard and Richard Haber, and Mary Jo Reiff argue that the explicit teaching of genre develops students' writing abilities and critical consciousness by encouraging rhetorical flexibility and genre awareness. Students learn new genres and their rhetorical situations, experiment within genres, and both expose and critique the ideological dimensions of genres. The argument follows that by doing so, students can gain control over genres and work against their constraints (Coe). One of the goals set forth by these scholars, then, is to teach students how to analyze genres (identify rhetorical choices and moves) by "collecting samples of a genre, identifying and describing the context [including the rhetorical situation] of its use, describing its textual patterns, and analyzing what those patterns reveal about the context in which the genre is used" (Bawarshi 158). Another goal is to teach students how to critique a variety of genres by questioning and evaluating a genre to determine its strengths and weaknesses as well as its ideological import, such as issues of power (Devitt et al. 150). The final and overarching goal is that students can then use these skills when encountering, learning, and writing genres in academic courses as well as in jobs, hobbies, and many other realms of their lives.

Like other writing curricula, these recent calls for the explicit teaching of genre incorporate the belief that students should begin writing instruction within the familiar. For example, *Scenes of Writing: Strategies for Composing with Genres*, a genre theory based first-year writing textbook co-authored by Amy Devitt, Mary Jo Reiff, and Anis Bawarshi, outlines how to perform genre analysis and critique while providing specific writing activities and assignments. In a chapter on genre critique, the authors ask students to begin with genres they already use:

> Think about how the genres that you use might be changed to suit you better. Consider genres you use at work, in school, in your public life, or in your private life. Select one that you would most like to see change and briefly describe how the genre works currently, the specific changes that might make the genre work betterfor you, and what these changes would achieve. (180)

At the end of the chapter, the authors also provide a writing assignment in which they use the word "familiar"; they ask students to "find a genre that you are familiar with and that usually is not longer than one page. Various forms fit this specification, but so do everyday genres like bills, obituaries, party invitations, and flyers" (183). Several genre scholars propose other methods for beginning the explicit teaching of genre within the familiar,[1] but when one of the goals of a pedagogy is to teach and develop critical consciousness (as it often is in many genre-based pedagogies), beginning with the familiar may not be the only effective approach.

Over the past five years, I have discovered that the unfamiliar, in addition to the familiar, may help students learn to analyze and critique genres and their rhetorical situations. When I first taught genre explicitly in my first-year composition classroom, I, like many others, began with the familiar. The first writing assignment, based on the suggestions in *Scenes of Writing,* asked students to select a familiar genre to analyze, critique, and then re-create. As the weeks progressed, I was pleased with the range of genres chosen and the level of genre and rhetorical analysis taking place, but I soon discovered that most students experienced difficulty when critiquing their chosen genres and corresponding rhetorical situations. For example, when considering what actions genres allow and do not allow their users to perform, when perceiving the ways in which genres succeed or fail, or when recognizing how genres limit their users' actions, students struggled and lacked critical insight.

One group of particularly avid sports players and fans consistently and adamantly presented me with an intriguing problem regarding their chosen genre of the sports ticket—"The sports ticket is perfect," they insisted, "It simply could not be changed." They argued it fulfilled its sole purpose of admitting them to a game. I kept asking them to consider other information on the ticket, such as seating, concession stands, advertisements, and legal ramifications regarding the reselling of tickets. I asked, "Does this other information serve no purpose? Does it not forbid certain actions?" But I was always met with the same, and slightly annoyed, response, "Of course, but it still just gets me into the game." This group was not the only one that experienced difficulty critiquing their genre. Regardless of genre, whether horoscopes, billboards, scoreboards, advertisements, music reviews, movie reviews, box scores, or embarrassing moments (popular in teen magazines), each group often insisted, "It works as it is; why would we want to change it?"

Student reactions like these are not limited to my classroom. Adrian Clynes and Alex Henry, in their article "Introducing Genre Analysis Using Brunei Malay Wedding Invitations" (2004), find themselves in a strikingly similar situation. They discover that their students experienced success in analyzing the familiar wedding invitation, but "the students were less successful with the other more important aspect of the task namely, relating and explaining the language found in the moves to the purpose(s) of the moves and to the overall communicative purpose of the genre" (240). In other words, the students experienced difficulty seeing the rhetorical possibilities and purposes of the genre. Instead, Clynes and Henry encountered "bald statements of the type, 'The function of the Formal Invitation is to formally invite the reader'" (240). Like my students, their students also asserted that the wedding invitation genre serves only one primary purpose, to invite the reader to the wedding, and resisted seeing other purposes of the wedding invitation.[2]

We certainly are not alone—other educators experience similar moments of student resistance. C. H Knoblauch, for example, identifies the majority of students within the university as mostly "from the comfortable middle of the American middle-class" (12). Since most students occupy this position, he questions the plausibility of students engaging in critique of social structures and categories when "teaching in circumstances where there is a powerful self-interest, rooted in class advantage, that works actively, if not consciously, against critical reflectiveness" (19). More specifically, he asks, "What do my students have to gain from a scrutiny of values and conditions that work to ensure their privilege?" (19). For Knoblauch, many students are resistant to examining the conditions of their own lives (familiar territory) because its works against their own self-interests and privileges.

One situation, then, that educators who invite students to begin within familiar territory may face is student resistance. While compositionists like Knoblauch may certainly be right to locate resistance as a "student problem," I believe that we can and should also read student resistance as a possible "pedagogical or teaching problem." For instance, when Clynes and Henry examine their assumption that students should begin genre analysis with a familiar genre, they continue to identify their approach as a "great benefit to [the students]" despite their discovery of its weaknesses, mainly the students' lack of success with this other *more* important aspect of analysis, "relating and explaining the language found in the moves to the purpose(s) of the moves and to the overall communicative purpose of the genre" (240-41).

Genre scholars have also acknowledged that familiar genres may be difficult for students to analyze and critique. In *Writing Genres*, for example, Devitt advocates teaching genre awareness and beginning genre analysis and critique with familiar genres, yet she also suggests that "once [students] are full participants in the genre, resistance becomes more difficult (some say futile) and choices become less visible (some say invisible)" (196). In other words, when students analyze and critique familiar genres, their ability to resist their ideological forces and imagine different rhetorical choices within genres is difficult.

Perhaps Clynes and Henry's, Knoblauch's and my students demonstrated signs of resistance not because they could not or did not want to critique and analyze familiar genres and their rhetorical situations but because doing so is a difficult and potentially threatening act. When students begin analysis and critique with familiar genres, they might perceive those genres and their rhetorical situations as important and even necessary for their successes in various avenues of their lives (as Knoblauch suggests). While it may be fruitful to examine resistance in terms of students, perhaps it is time that we also consider resistance in terms of pedagogical methods and approaches. Doing so would require us to engage in the same activity that we ask students to perform and to question our own pedagogical methods and assumptions, not just our students.

The Genre Effect:
"But It Still Just Gets Me into the Game"

In addition to beginning writing instruction with familiar genres, something else appears to be influencing students' understandings of genre and rhetorical situation than what is currently addressed in rhetorical genre theory. The very nature of genre, which current genre scholars have delineated, acts to suppress students' awareness of familiar genres and their situations as rhetorically complex. I believe that considering what I am terming "the genre effect" in conjunction with previous rhetorical genre theory work on "the ideology of genre" may help to account for student reactions and to critique our own pedagogical assumptions about the familiar. Students, like all readers and writers, come with a set of assumptions about how all genres work that makes it difficult for them to see the complexity, multiplicity, and variation within a specific genre and its rhetorical situation(s).

Student resistance to fully analyzing and critiquing familiar genres and their rhetorical situations may be understood, in part, by considering the effect of their overall conception of genres, what I am terming the *genre effect*: the overarching idea of genre that affects how we understand all individual genres working.[3] The genre effect, as a mental construct, exists within users' minds and informs how they view, understand, and perform the conceptual system of genre. This effect operates on all writers at all times, whether or not they are consciously examining their texts for genres, though, of course, its effect is particularly troublesome for educators using genre to teach rhetorical analysis and critical consciousness. Part of the genre effect, I argue, emerges from at least four distinct assumptions and beliefs that people hold about the system of genre: 1) Rhetorical situations in which a genre exists are not just similar but equivalent; 2) a current and specific rhetorical situation becomes representative of all rhetorical situations in which the genre may occur; 3) genres achieve one primary action; and 4) rhetorical differences between individual texts within a genre are often inconsequential.

To begin, differences within rhetorical situations are often masked by the genre effect. In genre theory scholarship, the rhetorical situation is not conceived in terms solely of materiality, but, instead, "situations are social constructs that are the result, not of 'perception' but of 'definition'" (Miller 156). In this sense, one constructs rhetorical situations through one's performance of genres, so when people encounter a rhetorical situation, they respond to it based on the genres that are available to them. Yet no two rhetorical situations are identical; every time a student attends a sporting event, the situation is different—it is another game, another date, another time, another sport, etc. But despite these differences within rhetorical situations, "recurrence [is] perceived by the individuals who use the genre" (Devitt 21). Users perceive different instances of the rhetorical situation to be similar, and I would argue, even the same, despite minor or major differences within them, such as settings, purposes, participants, and subjects. The likelihood of students distinguishing these differences— sometimes very slight differences—in rhetorical situations is diminished if the genre effect creates the illusion that variations within a rhetorical situation do not exist.

Moreover, as a result of masking these differences within rhetorical situations, the genre effect also works to hide the rhetorical complexity of the rhetorical situation. Users may feel compelled to view the current and specific rhetorical situation in which they are currently engaged and their position within it as representative of all the possible rhetorical situations in which the genre may occur. So even though a rhetorical situation may have many different participants, purposes, settings, and subjects, the genre effect collapses that complexity into simplicity. For instance, while I constantly encouraged students to consider more fully the rhetorical situation by examining the writers of sports tickets and other potential users, they continued to focus on their participation in the genre as sports players or fans. For this reason, analysis of the genre in conjunction with the rhetorical situation is often not enough to overcome the genre effect.

Another way in which the genre effect reduces complexity into simplicity is by masking the complex, multiple purposes of each particular genre and, thus, creating the belief that genres achieve only one primary action. Within rhetorical genre theory, genre is, generally, understood as "sociorhetorical habits or rituals that 'work,' that get something done, that achieve desirable ends" in a social context (Paré 60). For example, the sports ticket (genre) allows its users to gain admittance ("desirable end") to a sporting event (social context). Yet regardless of the multiple other social actions the genre achieves, users often perceive the sports ticket as performing *a* typified social action. They overlook other social actions that the sports ticket also achieves, such as controlling sale and distribution, promoting the consumption of concessions, or creating the status of the sporting event. Since other social actions do not forbid or interfere with users' "desirable end," admittance to the game, users are likely to neither see nor consider nor care about other positive or negative effects as long as the genre creates *a* primary positive effect for its users. Since genres provide meaning and focus for complex rhetorical situations users encounter every day (Bazerman, "Life" 23), they allow us to forget and avoid all the complexities surrounding our admittance to a sporting event, such as security, ticket sales, or seating. As a result, users may not feel compelled to consider other social actions a genre may achieve because the genre effect renders them not only less visible but also as unimportant or inconsequential for the primary social action to occur.

The genre effect also creates the illusion that rhetorical differences (such as content, format, structure, language, etc.) within individual instances of a genre are insignificant, especially for the main social action to occur. In my class, the sports ticket group collected many visually distinct tickets with a variety of information—some were in color, others in black and white; some contained advertisements; and some were much larger or much smaller than others. These differences, which certainly allow other social actions than merely admitting the students to the game, appeared unimportant as long as they still got the ticket holder into the game. In spite of differences within genres and the choices available to their users (as explored by Christie), the genre effect creates the perception that these differences and choices are irrelevant. In other words, even if we can see differences within a genre, those different instances still help to achieve the same (and valued) "typified rhetorical action." Regardless of shape, size, or color of the ticket, these different instances did not interfere with students' entrance into the game. And if the genre effect reinforces the belief that differences between instances of an individual genre do not matter for the primary social action to occur, asking students to locate and consider the effects of those differences certainly constitutes a difficult task.

The genre effect, then, is the overarching idea of genre in users' minds, and this overarching idea of genre reflects the beliefs that similar rhetorical situations are equivalent, that a specific rhetorical situation is representative of all possible rhetorical situations, that genres achieve only one primary social action, and that rhetorical differences within the genre features are often inconsequential. People come to understand this conceptual system of genre and how genres work in these similar ways through their daily interactions and experiences with individual, textual instantiations of genres. For genres to work, as genre theorists have elaborated, people must treat individual instances as though they are repetitions of prior experiences, with a purpose in common with other seemingly different individual instances. So genres, no matter how diverse or dissimilar they might appear, share a common bond—they work to create and reflect an overarching idea of genre, the genre effect, in the users' minds, which then, in turn, informs how users interact with future genres. This overarching idea of genre works to disguise or mask differences within, and elements of, social actions, rhetorical choices, and rhetorical situations within individual genres, thus creating an understanding of genre that transcends yet does not supersede experiences with individual genres.

In this light, the genre effect may account for why so many are willing to reduce genres to rules or formulas. If people generally reduce the rhetorical complexity of genres and their corresponding rhetorical situations and understand both as variation-free, then of course they would de-contextualize genres and conclude that every instance of an individual genre could be captured within a formula and that they can construct a genre based on its formula. And if the genre effect masks the complexities and variations within genres and rhetorical situations and allows users to go about their daily lives with little thought about how they are achieving their goals, then why would users and students possibly want or need to consider the complexities of genre and their rhetorical situations if they help users achieve their desirable ends? Students may have resisted critiquing familiar genres not only because of their investment in those genres but also because the genre effect masks the complexity of genres and their rhetorical situations while also creating the belief that variations within genres and their rhetorical situations do not matter, especially for the primary social action to occur.

In addition to the genre effect, previous work on the ideology of genre helps to account for student reactions to critiquing familiar genres. Many past and current genre scholars have examined how individual genres, genre sets (Devitt) or genre systems (Bazerman) create and reflect assumptions and beliefs of a social group, power, or institution within particular contexts. These assumptions and beliefs, then, affect the way those genre users view and interact with the world. While much scholarship has been interested in what kinds of actions genres allow, recent scholarship has focused on the ideological components of genres, specifically addressing what actions genres forbid or discourage and how genres constrain users' actions and create controlled subject positions for their users. For example, by examining a student essay within a women's studies course, Gillian Fuller and Alison Lee argue that the performances an individual genre (the student essay) position users (Ripley, the student) as certain kinds of generic subjects (student-subject, feminist-subject). Generic subjects are not formed prior to their performance of genres; rather "performing a genre concerns a joint agreement to perform certain positionalities within an institutional regime—to 'be' or 'become' certain kinds of subjects" (215). In other words, when users perform genres—either as a writer/speaker or a reader/listener—they take on pre-determined specified roles, mentalities, beliefs, and, thus become inculcated into the specific genre's ideology. Users then are not only positioned as certain kinds of generic subjects when performing a genre but are also positioned within the larger social apparatuses (University, Women's Studies, Feminism) that figure into the construction of the subject.

If the genre effect is paired with the work that exposes the ideological constraints of individual genres, then the picture I have painted thus far appears bleak. Genre is an even more complicated and messy system than previously theorized and imagined. If individual genres' ideologies shape users' actions (Ripley from Fuller and Lee's essay, for example) and the genre effect masks differences within and complexity of a genre and rhetorical situation(s), then achieving critical consciousness of genre seems exceptionally difficult.

I am not suggesting at this point, however, that the genre effect or our interactions with specific genres forbid the formation of critical consciousness within individuals, even though many might argue that critical consciousness is not achievable in any case since we can never sufficiently step outside of ideology. I believe that such a suggestion would deny the existence of individuals, presumably myself included, who possess the ability to be critical about a wide range of subjects. Many individuals develop the ability to be critical without the explicit teaching of genre; however, many of the students in my first-year writing course encountered difficulties. Most of us do. How, then, can composition instructors engaged in the explicit teaching of genre attempt to counteract the complacent positions we all find ourselves in during our less critical moments? My concern is how educators and students, together, can work against the genre effect and individual genres' ideologies in the classroom to foster critical consciousness.

The Explicit Teaching of Genre through the Unfamiliar

When educators engage in the explicit teaching of genre within the classroom, especially with the goal of critical consciousness, they need to consider both the genre effect and the specific genre's ideological components. Asking students to begin genre analysis and critique with familiar genres invites students to question their assumptions about genre (the genre effect) and also the ideologies of that specific genre. Although not impossible and often achievable, these are still challenging tasks. Students are often personally invested in the system of genre—genres do, after all, help people easily achieve their goals—and they are also personally invested in certain kinds of genres, as Knoblauch suggests. The sports ticket, for example, allows students easy access to the game, and the tickets represent a sport's ideology that those students already accepted. Familiar genres, therefore, also often reflect part of the individual, part of the "I." Asking students to begin a composition course by analyzing and critiquing familiar genres also often requires students to critique and question themselves. It is important, then, for compositionists to consider alternative approaches to the explicit teaching of genre, and one possible option that I outline here starts with the unfamiliar.

It may be useful to first isolate the genre effect so that students and instructors together can analyze and critique it before turning to familiar genres, like the sports ticket. Anthony Paré suggests that "genre's illusion of normalcy may be cracked or exposed at certain moments," such as when a "genre is stretched too wide, and its forms and actions are inappropriate or ill-suited to the occasion" or when "newcomers first begin to participate in genre and find it 'unnatural' or counter to their own discourse habits and aims (developed in school, for example)" (61). I would extend Paré's observation and argue that one way compositionists can force these "cracks" into their pedagogies is by inviting students to first analyze and critique unfamiliar genres and their rhetorical situations in order to isolate and expose the genre effect (the illusion of regularity and similarity). In other words, the genres that educators select for students to analyze and critique can be ones the students have not regularly performed in their daily and academic lives.

When students examine unfamiliar genres, they are most likely not already inculcated into the ideologies of individual genres, especially since they are not full participants in the genre. Moreover, students may not desire to become full participants in the genre since it seemingly lacks practical relevance in their daily lives. The lack of familiarity and desire might allow students to resist, even if just momentarily, indoctrination into an individual genre's ideology. If this resistance does occur, the possibility of isolating and uncovering the genre effect becomes greater; and if the genre effect can be isolated within the classroom, then students may be able to begin to question and examine it.

In my own classroom, I have asked students to explore the unfamiliar through historical and cross-cultural samples of genres. Many genre scholars already examine the historical progression of certain genres (see Popkin's examination of the resume, Bazerman's discussion of the U.S. patent, and Jamieson's exploration of the State of the Union and papal encyclicals). If genre scholars see the merit in examining genres historically, certainly students could benefit from such examinations as well. And while the proposition of examining genres cross-culturally has not yet been as popular an avenue for genre scholars, I have found that it works in a similar fashion to examining genre historically within the composition classroom.

While the focus of this essay is not necessarily on my own pedagogical methods (instead, I hope that I have laid some theoretical groundwork within which others will experiment), I do want to briefly explore what did take place in my first-year writing classroom to illustrate what the pedagogical stance that I advocate might look like. For several semesters, students have begun my first-year composition course by researching, collecting, analyzing, and critiquing historical and cross-cultural genre samples. While I provide students with several options, including loyalty oaths, campaign posters, war advertisements, playbills, census documents, political cartoons, wanted posters, and circus posters (of course, many other options exist), and sources in which to locate those genres so that I can guarantee the availability of samples, I have consistently been impressed with their range and variety of samples. Some examples include loyalty oaths ranging in topics from Hitler's and the Kamikaze Oath to a Stem Cell Research and a Bush-Cheney Voting Oath. Other students located Russian, British, Canadian, Australian, Chinese, and American War posters from the Civil War to the Iraq War.

Most students, of course, have encountered these genres sometime in their lives, but most have not regularly performed these genres as writers or readers. And even though students may have occasionally encountered these genres, they become unfamiliar when placed within historical and cross-cultural contexts. For example, examining campaign posters or war advertisements from other cultures—or from other time periods—changes the context (including the rhetorical situation) and the genres themselves in significant ways so that these genres become unfamiliar, even strange. Moreover, historical and cross-cultural genres have little to no practical use for students because the samples exist in cultural or historical contexts that differ considerably from the contexts in which students regularly operate. Since the practical, everyday use of the genre is diminished, the students and I can focus our attention on matters other than solely genre acquisition, proficiency, and production, such as analysis and critique.

Once students have collected samples, they begin the process of genre analysis, paying particular attention to how rhetorical features—including content, format, structure, diction, sentence structure, and rhetorical appeals—within a genre have changed over time within one culture and/or vary between different cultures. For their first writing project, I ask students to first compose, as a group, an annotated bibliography of their genre samples in which they describe two rhetorical features that they found to be most significant or revealing and briefly evaluate those genre features by discussing their significance (for example, what might the content, format, diction, etc. tell us about what the users value?). I then ask each student to compose an individual essay in which she [1] provides a comprehensive overview of the existing rhetorical choices or options of one genre feature, [2] creates three future rhetorical possibilities of that genre feature, and [3] identifies a present-day rhetorical situation in which the genre would be used and discusses which rhetorical choice within the genre features a writer would make in that situation (See Appendix 1). This essay is far from traditional (or even familiar) in the first-year composition classroom, but the primary goal here is to allow students to explore the many ways in which the rhetorical features in genres can and do change, often quite dramatically.

In this first writing assignment, students seem to be more willing and able to describe and imagine the possibilities of rhetorical choices within a genre because the variations in rhetorical features are more pronounced in historical and cross-cultural samples of genres than in samples from the same time period and the same culture. For example, one student examined the differences within diction across historical samples of American campaign posters. She found that campaign posters employ patriotic terms ("liberty," "loyalty," "democracy," and "free"), economic terms ("prosperity," "money," and "prestige"), alarmist terms ("public safety" and "DANGER"), or personal pronouns ("you," "you're," and "I") based upon the candidate's primary emphasis or message in the poster. Another student examined images (as part of content) within war advertisements to find that earlier images (often drawings) included presidents, rulers, or the political leader, whereas more recent war advertisements use images (often photos) of "everyday people working and fighting for their country." In addition to highlighting differences within genre features, this assignment also begins the process of connecting genre to rhetorical situation by essentially inviting students to become writers of the genres and make rhetorical choices based upon their created rhetorical situations. For example, the student who examined campaign posters decided that within a highly contested campaign, a current poster that would be located in someone's yard should use more shocking or alarmist diction to attract drivers or walkers passing by. While this was not the primary emphasis in this project and we did not focus on it within class (nor did the students in their essays), my hope was that students would begin to heighten their awareness that genres can and do change in response to contextual and situational elements (a process that is furthered emphasized within the second writing project).

Once students acknowledge in the first writing project that genres can and do change, they begin to discuss more explicitly why those changes might happen by considering how the context and rhetorical situations and, correspondingly, the social actions of the genre have changed. The second writing project builds on the first by asking students to locate a rhetorical feature(s) that has changed within their genre samples and speculate about the possible historical or cultural reasons for why that change(s) took place (See Appendix 2). In other words, if the genre features have changed, then they changed for a reason, and students are asked to connect changes in rhetorical features to changes in context and rhetorical situation. For example, some considered why the content or diction or images in a campaign poster from the 1800's is different from one in the 1900's. How might the rhetorical situations have been different? What kinds of different social actions are these two posters meant to achieve?

For this project, I do not provide students with extensive information regarding the historical or cultural contexts for their genre samples, nor do I require that they do outside research to fully discover those contexts (primarily due to time constraints). Instead, I ask students to speculate about what rhetorical situations the genres are responding to based upon the features that they have located within their genre samples. I believe that this is a possible task since, as Miller writes, studying genres "tells us less about the art of individual rhetors or the excellence of particular texts than it does about the character or culture of a culture or an historical period" (31).[4] I do recognize, though, that there is a possible danger in this aspect of the assignment: students may oversimplify the complexities of rhetorical situations and provide much too neat of an analysis. But my concern is not necessarily with having students get the rhetorical situations "right." Instead, I am more concerned that they see the relationship between genre and rhetorical situation and that they use their genre samples (often the only material artifacts that remain from certain cultures or time periods) to help understand and discern elements of their rhetorical situations.

That being said, I do know that students are not always merely speculating because most of the sources for the student samples provide contextual information that students can read (this is one benefit of providing sources for students to use). In addition, some students perform cursory research in to broadly understand the contexts of their samples. Another way to address this issue would be to ask students to consult Cultural Studies Readers that provide contextual information for various historical periods or cultures. Still, because I am ultimately asking students to speculate about possible historical or cultural reasons for change based upon their genre samples, we spend much time in the classroom discussing the importance of qualifying statements as well as exploring how to avoid stereotyping of historical periods or cultures by grounding their analysis within the genre samples. For example, we discuss the difference between providing concrete details from their genre samples to speculate about the rhetorical situation—such as "the image of Jimmy Carter leaning on a fence with the countryside in the background suggests that the voters may have been seeking a down-to-earth 'everyday man'"—and providing generalized statements about the context and rhetorical situation—such as, "During 1976, the country sought a down-to-earth 'everyday' man."

This second writing project invites students to see genres as intimately connected to rhetorical situations and contexts and to see how genres can and do change in response to rhetorical situations and contexts. The results of this project have been immensely fascinating for both me and the students. For instance, the student who looked at campaign posters found that her genre samples suggested that the "changes within rhetorical appeals are a direct reflection of what kind of leader or cause the country was seeking during various time periods." Another student examined loyalty oaths to find that "by examining these samples, one is able to see that over the course of time, the loyalty oath has become increasingly official in its content and format as a result of people's evolving dependency on proof of validity and completion of an oath." While these speculations may seem obvious (as in the first case) or may not be entirely "right" (as in the second case), students arrive at these speculations by analyzing the different rhetorical choices within their genre samples and seeking possible situational reasons for those choices. This second writing project also leads to the unforeseen benefit of allowing the class to focus closely on the composition and writing of the analysis paper itself, since students had already done the necessary genre analysis of their samples in the first assignment. We explored in-depth how to develop claims and subclaims, how to select and frame evidence, how to link evidence to claims and subclaims through analysis, and how to compose introductions and conclusions. These analysis papers, overall, were a success—so much so that a teaching mentor of mine at the time suggested that these were some of the best analysis papers that he had ever seen during a first semester composition course (and I agreed).

With a heightened awareness of the rhetorical features of a genre and their relationships to their rhetorical situations, I saw students begin to realize that differences in rhetorical features, social actions, and rhetorical situations are not inconsequential but important to the genre's performance. Once students began to acknowledge that genres do not have to be "simply the way things are," that genres do offer many possible social actions, that rhetorical differences do matter, and that rhetorical situations do, in fact, vary, the genre effect may have been diminished, if only momentarily. Moreover, with these experiences, students encountered fewer difficulties critiquing their unfamiliar genres. While the students implicitly critiqued their unfamiliar genres (at least critique is difficult to avoid) during the first two writing projects, we then briefly turned our attention to explicit critique, examining their unfamiliar genres for strengths, weaknesses, and ideological commitments. Critique seemed to be much easier when students could see patterns over time or ways in which genres have changed in order to accommodate inequalities, problems, etc.

The opportunity to at least partially expose the genre effect in the first two assignments opened the doors for critical examination of familiar genres. After students analyzed and critiqued unfamiliar genres, I invited them to select familiar genres so that they could analyze and critique them. My hope was that the first two assignments allowed students to develop some level of critical consciousness that would allow for the possibility for them to see their familiar genres as more than "simply the way things are." I did not anticipate a seamless transition nor did I expect one. However, students, on the whole, seemed to have a much easier time critiquing their familiar genres, as I encountered far fewer complaints and moments of resistance—(I did not once hear, "[the genre] works as it is; why would we want to change it?"). While no students selected the sports ticket, one student, an African American male athlete who spoke with me at length about his desire to become a professional track runner, did choose to analyze and critique posters for track. Through his critique, he quickly and easily discovered that the posters focused almost exclusively on African American male track runners, thereby portraying the idea that only African American males ran track—and ignoring female track runners, white male track runners, and other track runners of color. Of course, he may have arrived at similar conclusions if we had begun genre analysis and critique with familiar genres; however, my previous experience as well as other scholars' experiences indicates that he might have experienced difficulty doing so.

Reconceptualizing the Unfamiliar in the Composition Classroom

The pedagogical approach outlined here, which invites students to begin with the unfamiliar rather than the familiar, may seem counterintuitive, even contrary, to the current approaches that some compositionists, including genre scholars, use to foster students' critical consciousness. Students in my classroom did not begin genre analysis and critique with familiar genres, nor did they use familiar genres as a way into unfamiliar genres; rather they began genre analysis and critique with unfamiliar genres and used unfamiliar genres as a way into familiar genres.

I believe that the sequence of exercises, such as the one outlined above, allowed students to develop some level of critical consciousness and to develop their writing skills. In the first writing project, students gained the experience of locating the rhetorical features of their genres, defining them through a common vocabulary (content, structure, format, rhetorical appeals, sentence structure, and diction), articulating those features through detailed, written descriptions, and then using those features within later analysis (in the second project). Here, students learned how to locate and articulate concrete rhetorical choices and strategies used within genres, which provided them—and us as a class—with a common language or vocabulary for talking about writing (others and their own). The second writing project furthered students' writing abilities to develop claims and subclaims and support them with detailed evidence and substantial analysis, common rhetorical strategies used within academic writing. And through developing those claims and subclaims, many students recognized that genres can and do change in response to contexts and rhetorical situations and that genres often achieve more than one social action. Many students transferred the skills that they learned when examining unfamiliar genres to their examinations of familiar genres and experienced far fewer moments of difficulty and resistance while doing so.

I willingly admit that my pedagogical approach did not miraculously solve all problems or entirely eliminate moments of student resistance. Certainly the processes of developing critical consciousness and writing skills are not easy or seamless tasks. Students may need several courses, much more experience examining historical and cross-cultural genres, or much more practice analyzing and critiquing both familiar and unfamiliar genres and their rhetorical situations to fully develop their abilities. And other options already exist within the explicit teaching of genre. For example, Sarah Andrew-Vaughan and Cathy Fleisher use an "unfamiliar-genre research project" (2006) in which they invite their high school and pre-service teaching students "to investigate a genre of writing that they find challenging or unfamiliar, recognize the characteristics that define the genre, and then write an original piece in the genre" (36).[5] Another option may be found within Dylan Dryer's work where he suggests that teachers place students in uncomfortable (and unfamiliar) writing situations.[6]

In addition to the explicit teaching of genre, I imagine that other pedagogies would benefit by beginning within unfamiliar territory, especially pedagogies with the goal of developing critical consciousness. I see many other possibilities, and I invite others to experiment with the theoretical and pedagogical frameworks that I have provided here. Regardless of the pedagogical approach, beginning with the unfamiliar in addition to beginning with the familiar may help students develop critical consciousness within both unfamiliar and familiar territory as well as develop more control and insight into their own and other writing practices. And perhaps like our students, we, as compositionists, can also foster our own critical consciousnesses and develop insight into our own familiar pedagogical practices by turning first to the unfamiliar.[7]

Notes

1. Other examples can be found in Brooks; Brooke and Jacobs; Coe; and Reiff. Brooks draws on Bazerman's claim that "genres are the familiar places we go to create intelligible communicative action with each other and [are] guideposts to explore the unfamiliar," to argue that this statement "should be at the heart of a genre-based hypertext pedagogy" (342). He suggests that familiar genres help his students into the less familiar creative hypertext genre since "genres are the familiar places to which our students can go to compose in unfamiliar electronic writing spaces" (342). Brooke and Jacobs also seek to engage students in unfamiliar material through the use of familiar material. They explain that in their genre-based first-year writing courses, "students are invited to write frequently, to choose their own topics and genres, and to reflect on the many purposes, strategies, and uses of writing throughout their lives" and that "students . . . are encouraged to explore new *material* through genres familiar to them, but also encouraged to explore new *genres* using material familiar to them" (218).

   Coe proposes that students investigate a familiar topic by asking students to choose "a topic in which you have special knowledge" and then "communicate technical or specialized knowledge" to readers who are "moderately literate . . . and have little to no background in the specific subject matter" in the form of a brochure (164). Similarly, Reiff advocates that students perform mini-ethnographies in communities in which they are already participants (or ones in which they intend to become participants) to develop their understanding of genre as contextually situated.

2. Clynes and Henry offer a solution for fostering "students' ability to note and articulate the functional aspects of the analysis"; they suggest beginning with a "less complex homely genre" before analyzing more complex genres, such as the Brunei Malay Wedding Invitation (240). Less complex genres with their "less complex communicative purposes," they argue, would allow students to more easily see how the linguistic features relate to purpose (240). As I demonstrate, beginning with "less complex genres" (if such a thing exists) does not address the genre effect that helps to account for student responses like these.

3. I want to briefly explore how my theoretical concept of the "genre effect" differs from Bawarshi's "genre function" since, at first glance, they may seem similar. Bawarshi posits that the "genre function" allows us to study all kind of texts as "complex rhetorical actions that socialize their users into performing social roles and actions, roles and actions that help reproduce the realities they describe and enact" (357). In other words, all genres create participant

roles or subject positions for readers/listeners and writers/speakers, which users then reinforce and create through their genre performances. If genres "assign genre roles, both to the characters who participate within them to the writers and readers who interact with them" (347), then the genre function provides us with one way to examine how all individual genres establish genre-specific subject positions for their users.

The "genre effect" is also concerned with the larger system of genre that extends beyond individual genres and includes most, if not all, genres; however, it is concerned with the ways in which users come to view texts generically, not just the position that a given genre creates for them. Instead of claiming that all genres create genre-specific subject positions for their users, I claim that users come to understand how the larger system of genre works through their interactions with individual genres.

4. Miller goes on to provide an example: "Kaufer makes a telling point about classical Greek rhetoric when he observes that the 'number of definable types of rhetorical situations in Classical cultures appears both curiously small and stable' (1979: 176). The three Aristotelian genres signal a particular and limited role for rhetoric; according to Kaufer, but a very important one: maintaining 'the normal functions' of the state" (31).

5. Some unfamiliar genre examples they include are flash-fiction, cookbooks, microfiction, scrapbooking, sonnet, novel, and how-to books (32, 39). Asking students, as Andrew-Vaughan and Fleisher do, to select a genre they find "foreign or intimidating" (36), in other words unfamiliar, is another approach to the explicit teaching of genre that might enable students to examine the genre effect apart from the ideological effects of a particular genre.

6. Dryer asks students to compose either a first-person "project proposal" or a second-person "paper assignment" for a response paper prompt and then answer it after they had routinely composed eight response papers in response to his prompts (7).

7. Acknowledgements: I am especially indebted to Amy Devitt for her insightful comments on multiple versions and drafts of this piece as well as for her unwavering support and encouragement. I would also like to thank the anonymous reviewers for their careful readings and thoughtful suggestions. And I extend my appreciation to the many students who inspire me to be a better teacher and scholar.

Appendix 1

Writing Project 1: Tracing and Analyzing an Unfamiliar Genre

Goals: To collect primary evidence, practice genre analysis (as explored in Scenes of Writing), and use that genre analysis in your own writing.

Tasks: This project involves both a group and individual component. For both components, you should consider your readers (audience) to be members of the class and others already familiar with key terms.

Group Component: Each group will select a genre from the list provided and collect 9 (groups of 3) to 12 (groups of 4) historical (genres from various time periods) and/or cross-cultural (genres from other cultures) samples of your chosen genre. It is important that your group collects a wide range of samples from many different time periods and/or cultures. You will want as much variation as possible, so the following parameters apply:

1) No more than 1 sample from the United States in the last 25 years;

2) Samples cannot be from one time period (the early 1900s, for example) or from one culture (for example, France). In other words, you need either multiple time periods or multiple cultures;

3) Samples must be from at least three different sources.

Your group will then work together to identify and analyze the scene and rhetorical situation of the samples and to compose an annotated bibliography in which you perform a genre analysis of each sample.

Individual Component: Each group member will compose a 2-3 page response in which he or she:

1) Describes the existing choices of one genre feature (format, structure, content, diction, etc.) in all (9 or 12) of your samples;

2) Describes three future possibilities of that genre feature (choices that currently do not exist but might in the future);

3) Identifies and describes one possible rhetorical situation (partici-

pants, subjects, settings, and purposes) a present-day writer may encounter when using this genre (for example, running for a local political office, protesting a public education reform, enlisting in the United States air force, advertising a brand new off Broadway play, etc.)

4) Explores what genre feature choice (one of the existing and future possibilities you identify in the paper) this present-day writer may select in this rhetorical situation and why he or she would make that choice over other possible choices.

Appendix 2

Writing Project 2: Analysis of an Unfamiliar Genre

Goal: To create an analysis paper about your genre samples using sub-claims, evidence, and analysis to support your controlling idea (thesis).

Tasks: You will begin by considering what you find interesting, revealing, or strange about the genre features (content, format, diction, structure, etc.) in the sample genres that your group collected. Make sure you have received copies of your group members' annotated bibliography entries and genre samples. For example, you may consider what significant genre features changed in the samples over time and/or in different cultures. You could examine more than one genre feature in just a few (two-three) diverse samples, or you could select one feature to examine in several samples—the choice is yours. From this initial exploration, you will want to develop a controlling idea that speculates about the possible historical and/ or cultural reasons (scene and situation) for *why* the genre feature change(s) took place. In your controlling idea, you will want to demonstrate (make a claim) *why* the genre feature(s) change throughout history and/or in different cultures. Then construct an analysis paper with sub-claims, evidence, and analysis that explains and demonstrates the controlling idea.

Works Cited

Andrew-Vaughan, Sarah, and Cathy Fleischer. "Researching Writing: The Unfamiliar-Genre Research Project." *English Journal* 95.4 (2003): 36-42. Print.
Bawarshi, Anis. *Genre and the Invention of the Writer.* Logan: Utah State UP, 2003. Print.
Bazerman, Charles. "The Life of Genre, the Life in the Classroom." Bishop and Ostrom, 19-26. Print.

———. "Systems of Genres and the Enactment of Social Intentions." Freedman and Medway. 79-101. Print.

Bishop, Wendy, and Han Ostrom, eds. *Genre and Writing: Issues, Arguments, Alternatives*.Portsmouth: Boynton, 1997. Print.

Brooke, Robert, and Dale Jacobs. "Genre in Writing Workshops: Identity Negotiation and Student-Centered Writing." Bishop and Ostrom, 215-28. Print.

Brooks, Kevin. "Reading, Writing, and Teaching Creative Hypertext: A Genre-Based Pedagogy." *Pedagogy: Critical Approaches to Teaching Literature, Language, Composition, and Culture* 2.3 (2002): 337-56. Print.

Christie, Francis. "Genre as Choice." *The Place of Genre in Learning: Current Debate*. Ed. Ian Reid. Melbourne, Australia: Deakin University Centre for Studies in Literary Education, 1987: 22-34. Print.

Clynes, Adrian, and Alex Henry. "Introducing Genre Analysis Using Brunei Malay Wedding Invitations." *Language Awareness* 13.4 (2004): 225-42. Print.

Coe, Richard M. "'An Arousing and Fulfillment of Desires': The Rhetoric and Genre in the Process Era." Freedman and Medway, *Genre* 181-90. Print.

———. "Teaching Genre as a Process." Freedman and Medway, *Learning* 157-69. Print.

Coe, Richard, Lorelei Lingard, and Tatiana Teslenko, eds. *The Rhetoric and Ideology of Genre: Strategies for Stability and Change*. Cresskill: Hampton, 2002. Print.

Devitt, Amy J. *Writing Genres*. Carbondale: Southern Illinois UP, 2004. Print.

———, Mary Jo Reiff, and Anis Bawarshi. *Scenes of Writing: Strategies for Composing with Genres*. New York: Pearson, 2004. Print.

Dewey, John. *Interest and Effort in Education*. Boston: Houghton Mifflin, 1913. Print.

Dryer, Dylan. "'You Had to Separate a Lot to Get to the Basis of What You Know': Harnessing Genre Uptake for Genre Reflectiveness." Conference on College Composition and Communication Convention. San Francisco. 11 Mar. 2009.

Freedman, Aviva. "Show and Tell? The Role of Explicit Teaching in the Learning of New Genres." *Research in the Teaching of English* 27 (1993): 222-51. Print.

———. "Situating 'Genre' and Situated Genres: Understanding Student Writing from a Genre Perspective." Bishop and Ostrom, 179-89. Print.

Freedman, Aviva, and Peter Medway, eds. *Genre and the New Rhetoric*. London: Taylor, 1994. Print.

———. *Learning and Teaching Genre*. Portsmouth: Boynton, 1994. Print.

Freire, Paulo. *Pedagogy of the Oppressed*. New York: Herder, 1971. Print.

Fuller, Gillian and Alison Lee. "Assembling a Generic Subject." Coe, Lingard, and Teslenko, 207-24. Print.

Knoblauch, C.H. "Critical Teaching and Dominant Culture." *Composition and Resistance*. Ed. C. Mark Hurlbert and Michael Blitz. Portsmouth, NH: Boynton/Cook, 1991. 12-21. Print.

Jamieson, Kathleen M. "Antecedent Genres as Rhetorical Constraints." *Quarterly Journal of Speech* 61 (Dec. 1975): 406-15. Print.

Lingard, Lorelei, and Richard Haber MD "Learning Medical Talk: How the Apprenticeship Complicates Current Explicit/Tacit Debates in Genre Instruction." Coe, Lingard, and Teslenko, 155-70. Print.

Miller, Carolyn R. "Genre as Social Action." *Quarterly Journal of Speech* 70 (May 1984): 151-67. Print.

Paré, Anthony. "Genre and Identity: Individuals, Institutions, and Ideology." Coe, Lingard, and Teslenko, 57-72. Print.

Popkin, Randall. "The Pedagogical Dissemination of a Genre: The Resume in American Business Discourse Textbooks, 1914-1939." *JAC: A Journal of Composition Theory* 19.1 (1999): 91-116. Print.

Reiff, Mary Jo. "Accessing Communities Through the Genre of Ethnography: Exploring a Pedagogical Genre." *College English* 65 (2003): 553-58. Print.

Schryer, Catherine F. "Genre and Power: A Chronotopic Analysis." Coe, Lingard, and Teslenko. 73-102. Print.

Shor, Ira. "Educating the Educators: A Freirian Approach to the Crisis in Teacher Education." *Freire for the Classroom: A Sourcebook for Liberatory Teaching.* Ed. Ira Shor. Portsmouth: Heinemann, 1987. 7-32. Print.

Vygotsky, Lev. *Mind in Society*. Ed. M. Cole, V. John-Steiner, S. Scribner, and E. Souberman. Cambridge: Harvard University Press, 1978. Print.

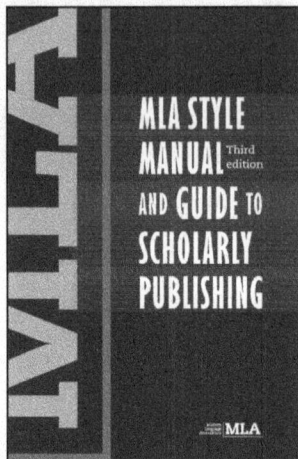

Everyday Curators:
Collecting as Literate Activity

Liz Rohan

In Mary Louise Pratt's oft-cited essay, "Arts of the Contact Zone," she argues that her son Sam's extracurricular hobby as a baseball card collector taught him about economics, racism, and American history, constituting literate activity that enabled him to hold his own in conversations with adults. Sam was also playing baseball at the time in Little League. While recognizing baseball's particularly "masculine ethos," Pratt celebrates her son's interest. School, Pratt adds, taught him "nothing remotely as meaningful to do" (33). Composition scholars have similarly noted that current college students are more engaged with self-sponsored activity such as Sam's baseball-card collecting than reading and writing for school. David Jolliffe and Allison Harl suggest, for example, that faculty members "create curriculums, co-curriculums, and extra-curriculums that invite students to engage in their reading and to connect texts that they read to their lives, their worlds and other texts" (613). In this article I take the positive view that our tasks as educators and human beings might not be to merely change what we do, but to re-see it. I think we should see ourselves most broadly as *collectors,* somewhat like Sam, who thus *already* engage in activities that can link personal and academic identities and practices, if over the long haul.

More emphasis on collecting as literate activity can also teach students to improve their thinking about primary sources and how selves, texts, and artifacts are constructed by culture. Collecting, annotating, and reflecting on collections can finally link the school activity Pratt chastises with the self-sponsored collecting activity she celebrates. To further these assertions, I analyze a variety of collections, including my own and those of my students. By sharing my own story of collecting along with my students' stories of collecting, I model how our similar enterprises and corresponding texts become yet another collection, a collection that undercuts assumed binaries and boundaries, such as those between teachers and students as well as between the personal and the scholarly. Throughout the article, I therefore "curate" a new collection that reflects a certain place and time. As Bruno Latour puts it, *"It is the sorting [of things] that makes the time"* (76). Although these stories of collections may seem disparate, each of them situates human beings as students and products of culture, a culture that invariably conflates public and private lives.

Collecting in Context

My burgeoning interest in the collecting process began when perusing the materials of the late Janette Miller, whose texts eventually became the topic of my Ph.D. dissertation. Born in Michigan's Upper Peninsula in 1879, this middle-class, white woman died in 1969 on the mountainous plateaus of Angola after a lifetime career as a missionary. During her long life, she amassed a variety of literate materials—several diaries, at least one scrapbook, personal correspondence, magazine articles, photographs, paintings, and poems. Many of these materials, both print and multi-modal, ended up in the archives at the University of Michigan's Bentley Historical Library, where I discovered them. Miller's collection of literacy materials are rich but limited and do not include the many texts she reportedly wrote and circulated in Africa, including those she wrote in the Angolan language, Umbundu.

I eventually organized my analysis around the main idea that Miller came of age during a profound transformation in American culture after World War I, when secular ideals usurped a largely Christian authority that had dictated a co-mingling of church and school in the nineteenth-century world of Miller's childhood. Miller rejected this transformed culture, living out her Christian identity in a remote African community she largely directed herself—and that once the aforementioned secular ideals made female-administrated missionary work no longer mainstream or fashionable. .

When analyzing the artifacts kept in the Chadds Ford, Pennsylvania home, (now turned museum), of the late Christian Sanderson, Teresa Barnett theorizes how an individual's collections can reflect his or her development of both personal as well as national identities, as does Miller's. Barnett describes Christian Sanderson, a sometimes teacher and educator in his community during his long life, as "[a] man with very little social or economic power" who was nevertheless "involved in myriad ways in public life and, on a local level at least, served as a transmitter of a national historical discourse that was very much a part of early twentieth-century Americans' understanding of themselves" (225). Sanderson's life as a collector, like Miller's life as a collector, teaches how the lives of ordinary individuals intersect with historical movements and ideas. When we engage in collecting, or in the analysis of collections, we invariably see how all lives are intertwined with a variety of so-called disciplines. For example, Sanderson's collection contains "[a] counting exercise done by his class when the school bell tolled for Woodrow Wilson's death," which symbolizes Sanderson's involvement with national discourse and mourning rituals. This object can be compared with a more personal relic, symbolizing mourning, that he kept to remember his deceased mother—"the string from the violin he played at [her] funeral" (233). Both of these objects show the intersection between Sanderson's personal and public identities as an American citizen and son. Of course, not all collections are equal. Some collections are undertaken consciously for an overt and culturally clear purpose—as with arranging photos in a photo album to tell a story, to remember, and to serve as a complement to other activity—photography. Other collections might be more or less haphazard, undertaken beneath our level of awareness, as with a junk drawer or even an office bulletin board.

I liken my experience of interacting with Miller's collection to Sam's baseball-card collecting practice and also consider the parallels between the rewards of Sam's activities with those experienced by a man such as Sanderson over a lifetime. Sanderson no doubt gained some esteem when seeing how his collection intersected with history making, both inside and outside of his local community. Likewise, when making meaning out of Miller's life—studying and engaging with her texts: I began to see how individuals' discourses reflect their engagement with local as well as national events, just as a baseball card collector might see how the endeavors of a home team compare with other teams across the country and across time. Moreover, the idea of life as interdisciplinary was illustrated to me by the many disciplines I had to mine in order to understand Miller's texts—American history, feminist theory, Christianity, postcolonial studies, African Studies, diary studies, photography studies, quilt studies, and, of course, literacy studies.

Philosopher Kathleen Wider makes a similar observation when reflecting on the process of researching the life of her grandmother, August Wider, a renowned speaker of art history: "[T]o understand a life one must understand the social and political context within which it's lived, the familial history of the person as far backward and forward as possible, the dreams and accomplishments of the person, the other lives that connected and supported the life examined and so much more." She concludes that, ultimately, "it is a source of comfort to know that one belongs to more than oneself even in one's own self-identity and beyond the confines of one's lifespan. We are alone neither here nor in the grave" (72). Wider's observation that learning about and studying a deceased individual's collections, as well as the other texts that put these items in context, suggests that by living our lives, we are also living history. Our everyday interactions with events and places will someday be historical fodder to our descendents and to future generations, but, as museum studies scholar Thomas Schlereth asserts, "[b]oth history texts and history museums . . . subtly [suggest] that historical reality is found between the covers of a book or within the glass cases of an exhibition" (335). History-making as collecting, *a process*, challenges the notion of learning as static—or "under glass." When collecting and annotating collections, we can see how history is made up of moving agents that might be *trapped* under glass—people, their stuff, and the shifting contexts that give them meaning. Furthermore, studying texts and related objects as part of a collection showcases what Peter Medway calls "fuzzy genres." That is, a text produced for one context may later have a broader or different function when it is reused or repurposed and becomes a mnemonic artifact (12). My own collection of literate materials, which I will discuss next, also reinforces the main idea I have introduced thus far: collecting is a lifetime, identity-forming process that leads to new collections through annotation and can connect school, personal, and even professional identities.

Everyday Curators

My interest in collections came to a head a few years ago after I returned to the environment of my youth, the Detroit area, after being gone for sixteen years. After applying for seventy academic jobs across the country, I ended up getting a job at the University of Michigan-Dearborn located between the town where I grew up and the town where I went to college. I was home on every front. Returning to a place after quite a bit of time away led me to remember many people and events I likely would have forgotten entirely had I not moved back. My memory was also enhanced because I was now able to access some of the materials I left behind in a "shrine" at my parents' home: two shelves of a cabinet with all of my papers from grade school to college.

Once I bought a house, my parents were all too happy to give me memorabilia from my shrine, along with a trunk to put it in. When gaining access to these new materials from my shrine, I was amused and entertained to discover more memories breathing through them. My parents put the shrine into a single trunk—the trunk my mother once used for her own memorabilia and that she took to the Peace Corps when she was in her twenties. The fact that the items from my shrine fit perfectly into this heirloom resonates with Latour's notion that *things* have history as well as agency, as well as Medway's observation that a genre's efficacy and purpose can transform over time and when met with new contexts.

When I perused items from the shrine, now in the trunk, the most compelling souvenirs were those I had dismissed, texts about events I had entirely forgotten. In my senior year of high school, in addition to writing in my diary, I summed up the months on the back of the pieces of a big calendar. I had never re-read this writing until my recent perusal of the shrine items because this writing had not attracted me. It seemed kind of weird that I wrote on the back of the calendar pieces, and maybe I was hesitant to revisit more adolescent angst on top of what I read in my diary texts. I had been a reporter for the school newspaper, the *North Pointe*, my senior year. According to the "calendar diary," one day the advisor for the paper, Mr. Amberg, pulled me into the hallway and said I was the best writer on the paper and that I ought to write a column like "Ramblings of Flem," written by Dave Fleming, who had graduated the year before. In Dave's column, he discussed his trials as a varsity athlete and shared his beefs with the school administration's policies. His column came out every Friday. Dave was also a kind of love interest/personal nemesis of mine. I never wrote a column, I remembered then, worried that people would think I was trying to be "like Dave." I also read about a time when my friends Faye, Colleen, Lisa, and I sat up all night talking on the beach. After this talk, I decided that I could "always go to them" with something really tough. I ended up writing a poem about this night that was published in the high school literary magazine, *Eclectics*. It was cool to reread about these insights because Faye and Lisa are my friends again now that I have moved home. They live near me now. It also seemed like my instinct to sum up the month on the calendar pieces was like a column for myself. Perhaps I was not ready to "go live" with the things that were important to me—like friendship—in the newspaper. Or, I didn't know how to go about making my interests public or interesting to others as Dave had been able to.

I ascertain a local and historically situated story of gender in this collection—I backed down from a public identity as a writer even though such had been modeled for me by Dave. But he was a boy. The artifacts in this collection also embody intersections between school-sponsored literacies (writing for the school newspaper) and self-sponsored literacies (when school becomes a topic for diary texts). The collection therefore foregrounds a discovery forwarded by Kevin Roozen in a recently published case study about a college student, Angela, which traces the intersection between Angela's processes as a writer of a private journal and her work as a Communication major. As Roozen argues, "[D]iaries, personal journals, and scrapbooks have long been placed at a considerable remove from persons' academic writing" (12), but Angela's experience and her private and school artifacts suggest otherwise. My collection, like Angela's public and private documents, hints at the relationship between self-sponsored literate practices—diary writing and poetry writing, diary writing and newspaper column writing—as well as to more concrete connections between self-sponsored and school-sponsored literacies. I wrote about an academic event, talking to Mr. Amberg, in the private texts. These documents in my collections also demonstrate the concept of "fuzzy genres." Years later when I reread them, the calendar diaries continued to fulfill one of their larger purposes; they helped me to work out and think about issues of my identity as part of a larger habit of diary keeping. They also had a second function, serving as mnemonic artifacts, reminding me of a relatively significant event that I had forgotten about entirely—being asked to write a newspaper column like Dave's, a column that was original and well-liked. Moreover, these items encourage my continued identity as a writer, and my ongoing "competition" with Dave. Dave is now a sports writer and has written two books. I remain on his heels. He is a role model for me even in his physical absence, as he was during my senior year of high school.

The Curator of Communities

My recently honed role as curator of my childhood literate materials came in handy in the summer of 2005 when I got in touch with a childhood friend, Amy, who moved away from our block in suburban Detroit to Denver when we were eleven.

In an email she sent to many friends and family, she implied that she was going through a break-up, which motivated me to call her. We hadn't talked in twenty years. After talking to her, I went through some of my memorabilia to find letters she wrote me from Colorado over the years. There were only a few letters, but they covered a lot of ground, documenting Amy's life from sixth grade through college. I recalled reading these letters years earlier and, when on the phone with Amy, had promised to send them to her because she lost a lot of her own memorabilia during her family's frequent moves. In one of the letters Amy wrote me when we were both about twelve, she said she wanted a puppy for Christmas, but her mother said no. Amy had no memory of this conversation with her mother, but found it funny since she now owns four dogs. Hence, items in my collection served as mnemonic artifacts for Amy as well, suggesting that when we collect for ourselves, we collect for others who share our culture, like Sanderson whose museum chronicles not only his personal history, but the history of his community and the nation.

While looking through these letters from Amy, I also found an old school assignment for a psychology class in my sophomore year of high school: a list of "twenty things I want to do for pleasure before I die." This discovery further suggests more fluid boundaries between private and public texts as well as between self-sponsored and school literacies. It was interesting to see also that I more or less had done at least ten of the things on the list—which included becoming a writer, going to college at the University of Michigan, and attending graduate school in Chicago. As with Amy's conversation with her mother, and my conversation with Mr. Amberg, I have no memory of completing the assignment. But I do remember that our teacher, Mr. Keeney, never read our homework, which he called "word credits." Rather, we'd put our assignment at the edge of our desks, and if we had our name and the date properly written on the homework, he'd give it a big stamp, "Credit."

I do have a memory of a very sensitive day I was having—after all, I was sixteen—when Mr. Keeney did not stamp my work "Credit" because it hadn't the proper date on it or something. I cried openly, and he sent me in the hallway where we had a tense exchange which resulted in Mr. Keeney reluctantly, if not unkindly, stamping the word "Credit," and with a bit of drama in front of the class (he, obviously, was a behaviorist). After discovering this item buried for twenty-two years, I put it on my refrigerator, updated it, and had my parents and Amy write their list about what they wanted to do before they die. This activity had context for Amy, who had just moved to a new city and was starting her life over again to some extent. Mr. Keeney, the alleged audience for the original assignment, never touched it. It's even possible that this was the word credit I almost didn't get credit for. When it comes right down do it, even though he created the assignment, Mr. Keeney's response didn't matter at all. The item, like Amy's letters, had a greater destiny. Decades later, both Amy's letters and the word credit had persuasive power and arguably profound meaning. They aligned articulated goals with manifested destinies. As one of my students, Patty,[1] whom I'll quote again later, has said,

"Identity doesn't happen in a vacuum. Our choices are rooted in thought." Writing and reflecting on this writing can be "proof" that we live lives more fulfilling than we know. This writing and reflection can also get us on track, even back in touch with our past selves and perhaps with people who affirmed these past selves—as was the case with getting in touch with Amy during the summer of 2005 and also rereading the calendar diaries.

Again, these events further emphasize intersections between personal literacies and school literacies when artifacts from each "camp" are housed in one collection. They show furthermore how ordinary texts, even texts for school collected only somewhat consciously, can have a profound function, their contexts limitless. As Mikhail Bakhtin might argue about the efficacy of texts over time, "There is neither a first nor a last word and there are no limits to the dialogic context (it extends into the boundless past and the boundless future)" (73). Medway similarly critiques the assumption that a text can "be immediately communicative" because it "rests on an over simplistic understanding of social action" (143). The 1984 word credit assignment was not "immediately communicative." Its arguably more important meaning and audience would not be created for twenty years when the text inspired explicit "social action": discussion about the concept of twenty things you might do before you die and the production of more lists about such, and by people a bit closer to the grave who could better look backwards and forwards. The story of the word credit can illustrate how the audience and purpose of texts produced for school can transcend the boundaries of a classroom, when these texts are repurposed as mnemonic artifacts and sources for further text production.

The Personal Literacy Inventory

These discoveries from my own archives motivated me to create an assignment for my students asking them to peruse and make meaning from their own collections. I call the assignment the personal literacy inventory. This activity is particularly possible at a school like mine, a commuter college. Many students live at home, or close to home, and therefore have access to childhood memorabilia.

I have most recently introduced the concept of collecting as literate activity first by asking students to think about their personal music collections, assuming that all students would have some type of relationship with music, and because not every student has a collection of saved schoolwork. While doing so, we read two published essays about music by two very different "curators." In his essay, baby boomer John Rosenthal "annotates" his personal 1950s record collection, at first nostalgically and then critically, when he notices how the songs of his boyhood day were more saccharine than he had remembered and also encouraged unrealis-tic scripts about romance. He asks himself if "the music that introduced [him] to American popular culture . . . offered him a place to hide from more demanding claims of self" (19). His analysis, like the story of Sanderson's collection, also

CREDIT

Liz Baker
Psychology
9-19-84

20 activities I'd want to do for pleasure
before I die

Every day - 18,000

F = physical or mental risk   once a year - 60

R = release of physical energy   once a month - 720

L = love - "oneness"   once a week - 3000

G = dealing with grief or the past

1. Write a short story that will make the reader cry. 60 F.L.
2. Attend college at U of M 18,000 F, L
3. Attend graduate school at Northwestern University 18,000 F
4. Tour England, France and Ireland to meet people that represent the character of the countries 60 L
5. Be a reporter for the Chicago Tribune 18,000 F.L.
6. Be a reporter for the New York Times 18,000 F.L.
7. Be a writer and/or editor for a New York fashion magazine big-city 18,000 F.L
8. Decorate a downtown, luxury apartment. 60 L A.
9. Buy a country home with enough land for horses and a big garden 60 L
10. Drive a luxurious sports car that is my very own 18,000 A.G L.

"We'd put our assignment at the edge of our desks, and if we had our name and the date properly written on the homework, he'd give it a big stamp, 'Credit.'" (Above)

"One of my student's, Henry's, personal literacy inventory, an analysis of a comic book, demonstrates how the annotation of a personal collection can be mnemonic and can also help students better recognize how their choices are constructed by culture." (Right)

shows readers the intersection between personal and cultural identities. Rosenthal's actions and worldview as a boy and teenager were influenced by the music he listened to, the scripts he was assigned. Writer and scholar Paul Lauter is even more incredulous about his relationship with cultural scripts when discovering his post-World War II junior high songbook, a notebook of popular songs that students illustrated. These artifacts show Lauter how identities were prescribed to him by dominant American culture. He was inevitably complicit in the construction and distribution of these identities when engaging with songs about war, manliness, and Christianity, the last being ironic considering that Lauter is Jewish. Lauter's discovery is yet one more example of "fuzzy genres," when schoolwork acts as a mnemonic artifact, and in this case embodies a different kind of lesson about culture than Lauter's junior high teacher planned fifty years ago. Composition scholar Morris Young makes a similar observation about cultural scripts and his identity as an Asian American when analyzing the context of items in his personal collection, including the records about his progress with a speech pathologist, his first library card, and items he produced in preschool. For Young, these artifacts represent prescribed cultural scripts that align literacy with economic mobility and American citizenship but in tension with the "linguistic discrimination" faced by his minority parents in Hawaii (23).

After reading these essays about Rosenthal and Lauter's collections, students are better equipped to look "critically" at their own music collections, and similar materials, to see how their choices have been constructed by culture, particularly during their pre-teen years. Many girls, for example, write with horror about their former "boy band" obsessions, evidenced by artifacts in their home music collections. Lauter's piece also helps students consider how their schoolwork is a kind of relic from which they can garner perspective about culture and prescribed dominant values. Most of all, these articles invite students to consider themselves as collectors who own and produce primary sources that can be "fodder" for scholarly analysis. Hence, curators are born.

Student Examples: The Personal Literacy Inventory

One of my student's, Henry's, personal literacy inventory—an analysis of a comic book—demonstrates how the annotation of a personal collection can be mnemonic and can also help students better recognize how their choices are constructed by culture. Henry produced the comic book outside of school when he was nine. Reflecting on its production reminded him that reading and producing comic books was not a valued literate endeavor in his scholastic past, a trend he aimed to buck when an educator himself in the future. Henry had fond memories of producing this book and was surprised, both pleasantly and otherwise, when revisiting the text. As he describes the experience, "I picked up the stack of nine yellowed pages and nostalgia instantly set in . . . I remembered the story as being great. I was afraid, even at my age that the story would not live up to how I remembered it. Unfortunately I was right." For one, he named his character the "Inihelator," with an I instead of an A. He had sounded out the word phonetically. He recalled the comic as penned by the hand of original genius, but in revisiting it saw that his plot and character development relied on the tropes of common comic heroes. For example, his Inihelator is a lawyer as is the Marvel comic hero, Daredevil. Inihelator's costume is also conventional in design and color. The plot jumps around, the villain is poorly developed, and, as Henry said, "the whole seven-page story is essentially one huge paragraph. Punctuation is present, but often incorrect."

Despite its flaws, Henry writes:

> I'm proud of Inihelator. At the age of nine, I created a hero, a story, and something that makes me smile whenever I think about it. My main issue with the story is that it remains unfinished. What did I want to write after the final sentence? How was the story going to end? Was the story going to end? What was nine-year-old [Henry's] main goal? I guess I'll never know my story would have led. Maybe that's okay. Maybe that leaves a starting point for me to continue the (albeit short) legacy of the Inihelator. Maybe I'll be able to collaborate with my nine-year-old self in order to further Inihelator. Someday, when the time is right and the world needs a new hero, a new savior, a new champion, the Inihelator will be reborn.

Just as Henry was reminded of his passion for comic books when a young boy, another student, Wendy, revisited her deep and long interest in language when annotating her collection of schoolwork and its gem: a book of nouns she wrote for a school assignment in third grade. As a current Linguistics major, she regarded this discovery of the noun book in her collection as both humorous and prophetic. She describes the experience:

> One of the things that struck me in looking through my mom's folder of my childhood is my obvious interest in language. I distinctly remember making my "Nouns" book and being very careful not to confuse the different types of nouns there are. I took a concerted interest in seeing to it that each type was represented and identified in its own right. I also remember I wanted very badly to make my "word book" make sense. I wanted each page to have a complete sentence instead of just words. It didn't feel right to me to have words in random order. These assignments probably seemed so trivial in third grade when I was doing them, but looking at them now with my adult eyes, I can see how important they were. I suppose, then, it's not surprising that I now work as a tutor and proofreader for students of English as a second language making sure that their words are all in the right order and make sense.
>
> As I got through my mother's saved memories of my childhood, I realize that saving my schoolwork is very important. I see pieces of my past that are very directly linked to my present. It's as if those ties had become

so familiar and so understood that they just faded into the background. Looking through them now has helped bring them back to the foreground, has painted them in bright colors again.

Wendy's observation that her earlier choices as a writer foreshadowed or even reflect her contemporary identities parallel Mark Leone and Barbara J. Little's claims about museum collections: "Making connections among artifacts and between our genealogies and artifacts, therefore, is one way of exposing origins and laying claim to history" (370). Indeed, Wendy was able to "make claims with history," her own history, by perusing previous schoolwork. Wendy's analysis of her noun book in context with her earlier and persisting interest in language echoes Young's observation about his similar early interest in language, which he reflects upon when undertaking his own type of personal literacy inventory. As Young puts it, "As I reflect back on my life it is not surprising that some of my most vivid memories of my childhood are about language" (20). For Wendy and Young, saved items are material sources that document their experience with school and literacy, draw attention to their persistent aptitudes, and put their career choices into a greater context.

Another one of my students, Patty, had a similar experience to Wendy when conducting a personal literacy inventory. Patty made a collage of some writing she did for school and linked the texts with artifacts to represent the phenomenon that she had achieved some of the goals that she had put in writing years earlier. Ten years prior, she had written an informal paper for school that outlined her goals to be a teacher. These goals are still relevant as she pursues a teaching certificate in college. Of this discovery, she said, "You are the same person no matter. I'm still interested in all stuff that I totally forgot about. Identity is a bit more constant [than we might think it is]." In Patty's collections, she also found a journal entry she wrote for an assignment in school about her choice "to stay home and do homework instead of playing laser tag." Later she found a receipt from playing laser tag. Her artifact collection showed her the constancy of her values. The artifacts themselves, the journal entry and the laser tag receipt, evidence further how school and non-school activities can be fused enterprises for identity formation. These items also became mnemonic artifacts for her to consider the events that shaped her identity and the practices that encouraged her and allowed her to build and maintain this identity.

The writing she kept was "a concrete example of identity," Patty says, adding, we "don't see our 'selves'" every day. We might not "view ourselves as focused or motivated, always knowing what to do." Rosenthal notes how dominant values of his 1950s American boyhood were embodied in the artifacts he perused in his record collection, which in hindsight felt constricting, and he felt some ambivalence about his collection, as does Young when thinking critically about literacy as assimilation. For Patty, revisiting artifacts that she kept in her collections affirmed her goals and assured her that she was on the right track, or at least a thoughtful one. Just as my discovery of the word credit assignment led to the creation of a new collection—more lists—analyzing mnemonic artifacts also inspired Patty to create another collection, a collage of materials arranged to make explicit the links between her values and activities that were embodied in these artifacts. While young students like Henry, Patty, and Wendy obviously lack the long view afforded to scholars who study collections of the deceased or of older adults with more life experience, they can still benefit from critical distance as a tool, can see how they are products of culture, can "annotate" their materials with insights, and may use their reflections about their pasts to shape their futures.

The documents of one of my *historical* subjects, Enoch Price, who came of age years ago in the late nineteenth century as he completed law school at the University of Michigan and embarked on his legal career, also illustrates the potential of the "fuzzy genre," when texts become mnemonic artifacts over time. While Rosenthal, Lauter, and Young, as well as Henry, Wendy, Patty, and myself, have used personal artifacts to remember and look back on lived lives, Price used writing to help him predict the future. The year before he entered law school, in 1889, Price actually wrote himself a memorandum outlining his goals for the next five years and put it in an envelope to be opened after these five years had past. He wrote, "Today I am 25 years old. Have been thinking much the past few days of what my past life has been and what the future may be. Will write a little prophecy of the coming five years. I believe in peering into the future by nucleus of <u>self-study</u>." He classified "for brevity's sake" the categories of life he knew would fluctuate or he hoped to improve upon: physical, religious, social, professional, and geographical. Predicting his future performance in the social category for the upcoming year, 1890, he had written "not brilliant—too much in love. Propose (?)." Price was pretty good at this fortunetelling. Nearly a year later, he proposed to his former college friend, ongoing love interest, and longtime pen pal, Louise. Geographically he guessed that he'd be "in the office of a good attorney in a thriving town of 40,000 west of Mississippi" by the end of 1892. Upon graduating from law school in 1891, Price actually moved to Chicago, began work as a clerk, and eventually began his own practice shortly before he got married. So this young man did go west, just not as far as he thought he would. Price also came from a family obsessed with memorial. He and his brothers kept diaries, saved letters, calling cards, and related memorabilia, and worked together to write a family history. Price's father, an Ohio apple farmer who also ran a literary society, kept a diary for fifty years. Perhaps as a diarist Price learned that a present state of mind, if jotted down, can predict a future reality. Or, as Patty might put it, "Identity doesn't happen in a vacuum. Our choices are rooted in thought."

Conclusion

Henry writes about the possibility of collaborating with his nine-year-old self. He arguably is collaborating already with this self when talking back and forth with his artifact, the comic book. The same could be said of my friend Amy revisiting her love of dogs, of Wendy revisiting her love of language, of Patty revisiting her goals of being a teacher and finding balance between work and play, and of Enoch Price hoping to touch the future during a transitional period of his life. Collections as literate activity can link us to our past as well as to our future. Henry's comic and Wendy's noun book, for example, helped them see the genesis of their current values.

Collecting can also break down a strict distinction between production and consumption as literate activity when these artifacts act as mnemonics, such as Patty's laser tag receipt and the many items in Sanderson's collection. Curators of artifacts they have previously consumed become producers when they interpret artifacts in their collections and when these artifacts are used to develop narratives about selves and culture. Thomas Rickert and Michael Salvo associate this kind of reuse and "repackaging (of) content" with the "prosumer," a role that breaks down "the formerly separate categories of consumer and producer" (298). When remixing and repurposing items in a collection for a new end, such as remembering or storytelling, curators of collections like the ones described in this article act as "prosumers" of the items they analyze and arrange.

These samples of collecting as a literate activity also suggest a more fluid boundary than we often acknowledge between private and public texts, between texts produced for a school, like mine, Wendy's, and Patty's, and texts produced at home, like Henry's. When all texts become, for whatever reasons, artifacts in personal collections, their original context as private or public is often irrelevant. Just like Henry's Inihelator, they are waiting always to be reborn when rediscovered, reread, and repurposed. As Bakhtin might observe, "[E]very meaning will have its homecoming festival" (73). Secondly, while school methods might be understood stereotypically as the disembodied, decontextualized consumption of knowledge, or knowledge "under glass," as human beings, and in the long view, we engage in the production of knowledge that could be conceived as "scholarly" when simply making meaning out of our lives through the activities we choose to value, how and where we display artifacts representing them, and what they teach us about the culture we live in when we reflect on them. Finally, as several of these collections show, school assignments are often fodder for collections, and this work can profoundly shape lives and identities years after their original production.

Much of my pedagogy hinges on introducing my students to the efficacy of ordinary texts they produce for school, work, or pleasure. As mentioned, at the very least, by the end of the course students might value the texts they produced for my class as artifacts with limitless contexts, if saved, or in some cases just remembered as literacy events, as Henry remembered producing his comic book. I like how the stories of text production and the reflection of texts situate me, Amy, Wendy, Patty, and Henry as students of our selves and the life choices shaping these selves. I also like the discovery that texts composed by a nine-year-old, and even an angst-ridden sixteen-year-old, can inspire and even motivate others, and even grown-up others, when these texts meet new contexts.

If we conceive of ourselves as lifetime collectors of meaningful, history-making, and transformative activities, we might better link what we do in school to the research and identity-shaping activities that give our lives meaning when "at home." In other words, we might better see the liminal spaces connecting our "real-world" passions with both the materials and methods gained in formal school settings, and we might better understand ourselves as everyday history makers synthesizing complicated and competing discourses in an interdisciplinary world, every day, and all of our life. Having engaged with the personal literacy assignment myself, and having taught it, I've come to see the need for theories that better contextualize the life of texts in and beyond the classroom and, better yet, try to understand their function in shaping and building lives. I agree with Jennifer Sinor who "question[s] just how far we've come in reading the many ordinary things around us" (5). The academy would benefit by considering the production and reflection on texts, whether narratives about sports, comic books, or cataloguing nouns, as a collection process whereby the ultimate resting place and contexts of texts we assign remain mysterious, even as they bounce in our book bags prior to grading them, and long after a student has left our classroom.

Notes

1. As a common courtesy I have changed the names of the students whom I discuss, and partly to avoid confusion because two of the students have the same name!

Works Cited

Bakhtin, Mikhail. "Toward a Methodology for the Human Sciences." *Professing the New Rhetorics: A Sourcebook*. Ed. Theresa Enos and Stuart C. Brown. Englewood Cliffs: Prentice Hall, 1994: 40-62. Print.

Barnett, Teresa. "Tradition and the Individual Memory: The Case of Christian Anderson." *Acts of Possession: Collecting in America*. New Brunswick: Rutgers UP 2003: 221-235. Print.

Carbonell, Bettina Messias, ed. *Museum Studies: An Anthology of Contexts*. Oxford: Blackwell Publishing, 2004. Print.

Jolliffe, David A. and Allison Harl. "Texts of Our Institutional Lives: Studying the 'Reading Transition' from High School to College: What Are Our Students Reading and Why?" *College English* 70.6 (2008): 599-617. Print.

Kirsch, Gesa, and Liz Rohan, eds. *Beyond the Archives: Research as a Lived Process.* Carbondale: Southern Illinois UP, 2008. Print.

Latour, Bruno. *We Have Never Been Modern.* Trans. Catherine Porter. New York: Harvester, Wheatsheaf, 1993. Print.

Leone, Mark P., and Barbara J. Little. "Artifacts as Expressions of Society and Culture: Subversive Genealogy and the Value of History." Carbonell 362-74. Print.

Medway, Peter. "Fuzzy Genres and Community Identities: The Case of Architectural Students' Sketchbooks." *The Rhetoric and Ideology of Genre.* Ed. Richard Coe et al. Cresskill: Hampton Press, 2002: 123-53. Print.

Miller, Janette. Diaries, 1894-1909. Box 1. Papers of Janette Miller, Congregationalist Missionary to Angola. Bentley Historical Library, University of Michigan, Ann Arbor. Print.

Pratt, Mary Louise. "Arts of the Contact Zone." *Profession* 91 (1991): 33-40. Print.

Price, Enoch. Memorandum. Papers of Enoch J. Price, 1879-1945. Folder 16. Welsh (Licking Co.) Price and Related Families Genealogical and Biographical Collection, Ohio Historical Society. Print.

Rickert, Thomas, and Michael Salvo. "The Distributed *Gesmamptkunstwerk*: Sound, Worlding, and New Media Culture." *Computers and Composition* 23 (2006): 296-316. Print.

Roozen, Kevin. "From Journals to Journalism: Tracing Trajectories of Literate Development." *College Composition and Communication* 60.3 (2009): 541-573. Print.

Rosenthal, John. "Frankie and Perry and Patti and Dean." *The Sun* June 1999: 14-17. Print.

Schlereth, Thomas J. "Collecting Ideas and Artifacts: Common Problems of History Museums and History Texts." Carbonell 335-71. Print.

Sinor, Jennifer. *The Extraordinary Work of Ordinary Writing: Annie Ray's Diary.* Iowa City: U of Iowa P, 2002. Print.

Wider, Kathy. "In a Treeless Landscape." Kirsch and Rohan 66-72. Print.

Young, Morris. *Minor Re/Visions: Asian American Literacy Narratives as a Rhetoric of Citizenship.* Carbondale: Southern Illinois UP, 2004. Print.

(Un)earthing a Vocabulary of Values:
A Discourse Analysis for Ecocomposition

Paul Walker

The schismatic environmentalist Edward Abbey said, "developers and entrepreneurs must somehow be taught a new vocabulary of values" (85). Abbey's statement maintains the existence of strong relationships among words, beliefs, and actions, and for him, such relationships were crucial in his lifelong efforts to alter society's conceptions of how humans interact with their environment. From a rhetorical perspective, it is significant that Abbey did *not* say, "developers and entrepreneurs must somehow be taught new values." By emphasizing the vocabulary of values—how we talk about them—Abbey understands that how we communicate our values may be more important and influential than what values we think we hold. In this way, his brief statement helps us look beyond how "terminology constructs the conceptual categories through which people understand the world" to the rhetorical implications of how that terminology is generated and used (Allen and Sachs 572). A variety of legitimate societal constructs promote developers to speak of the environment in economic terms, but alternative value-constructs are also legitimate and justified. When these constructs clash, the underlying attitudes and values are often misunderstood as primarily internal—separate from our external language and the language of our society. This prevailing view has emboldened varying academic approaches—cognitive, epistemic, and social constructionist—that contend, in different ways, that the only way we discover what we believe or know is through our communication of it.

These approaches to the relationship between writing/communicating and learning/knowing are central to composition studies, enabling the "rhetorical turn" in our analyses of writers' social and physical contexts to look "beyond the individual writer toward the larger systems of which the writer was a part" (Hawisher et al. 65). In that vein, Sidney Dobrin and Christian Weisser encourage the combination of ecology and composition—ecocomposition—as a way to explore "the relationships between individual writers (identity) and local environments (ideology, space) as well as ways in which populations interact with environment (culture)" (18). Because of our keen understanding of the power of language as a meaning-making system, the field of Composition and Rhetoric is well-positioned to help students—future developers, entrepreneurs, and consumers—better understand the origins and potentials of their own identity, ideology, and culture: the catalysts for a vocabulary of values.

Therefore, I agree with Derek Owens in his promotion of the composition course as a "cross-disciplinary" location for which "sustainability-conscious curricula" is well suited (27). In addition, Peter Goggin and Zach Waggoner advocate the composition course as a location for English scholars and teachers to "take action" in worldwide efforts to promote sustainable practices (46). The key element for us to be active in such a role is our understanding of discourse as a meaning-making, rhetorical process. Dobrin and Weisser point out that utilizing rhetorical critique of environmental discourse and its multiple contexts to help solve disputes is not enough. Instead, "ecocomposition must look beyond environment as merely a thing about which we have disputes and about which discourse participates and creates, but as the very thing that the production of all discourse is reliant upon and contributes to" (46). The malleability of environmental and economic terms make issues of sustainability "wicked problems" (Rittel and Webber), because the values of various publics hinder resolution when there is inherently no "one-best solution." Nevertheless, while *sustainability* is often formulated as a solution to societal problems of energy consumption, "the information needed to *understand* the problem depends upon one's idea for *solving* it" (161).

The objective of this article is to propose an analytic method through which composition students and others might discover and understand the ecological complexities of prevailing environmental terminology that create "wicked problems." Through this method, students engage in "discursive ecology" by exploring the connections among discourse, people, and the environment with the intent to "produce writing" that addresses those contextual connections (Dobrin and Weisser 116-17). The close analysis of environmental discourse proposed here can provide students the opportunity to identify and critique the tacit societal values to which we adhere and how accepted language and labeling contribute to and inform the continuation of those values. As alluded to by Owens, much as the inclusion of texts exploring multiculturalism, race, class, and gender allows students to read and write about rhetorical and historical hegemony of culture, the study of sustainability likewise requires students to examine their understanding of the hegemony of progress (4).

In this article, I demonstrate an analysis of land-use conflict language that includes the essentials of what might be used in a composition classroom. The framework of analysis has a range of applicability for composition teachers, whether as a short-term or long-term assignment. The extent of how the analysis is used is less important than the recognition of the connections between language and values, and the understanding that environmental issues, large or small, are embedded in language. From the constructed definitions of our vocabulary to the manipulation of its terminology, "the environment" is founded upon and contested through rhetoric and discourse.

This opens up the textual and discursive opportunities for classroom study, for, in any community, city or county, it is likely that a number of land-use conflicts occur each year.

Furthermore, similar to Goggin's and Waggoner's sustainability-based composition course, the method of analysis that I advocate here also embraces the New London Group's multiliteracy pedagogy within contextual locations by providing *situated practice, overt instruction, critical framing,* and *transformative practice* (see Goggin and Waggoner; Cope and Kalantzis). Students participate in the typical elements of a composition course by identifying, researching, and writing about the rhetoric of land-use conflicts, yet the critical analysis situates that work within the social and environmental complexities of their hometowns or college towns.

Therefore, envisioning this as a class assignment or project, I recommend beginning by helping students choose a local land-use or environmental conflict—initiating the *situated practice* by collecting documents and accounts from all sides. Once a conflict is chosen by the individual student or class as a whole, students should be instructed on the framework of analysis, which has two parts: *term analysis* and *conflict-language analysis.* Along with the *critical framing*, instructors should also help students understand the philosophy of the assignment by reading and discussing essays or excerpts relating to how values, language, rhetoric, and meaning are intertwined purposely by humans for various means. Once the analysis, as shown below, is conducted and complete, students should submit formal papers that describe, explain, and argue the results, and time should be given for presentation of papers and class discussion in order to enable *transformative practice.* The remainder of this article follows my recommended order of assignment steps: I provide background on a land-use conflict, unpack and explain the framework of analysis, demonstrate the method and results of my analysis of this conflict, and conclude with a summation of how such analysis elucidates the complexity of values and society.

Sacred Land, Sacred Snow

From 1999 to 2007, I lived in Flagstaff, Arizona. This small city sits at the foot of the San Francisco Peaks, the highest of which rises over 12,000 feet above sea level. Flagstaff's elevation is around 7,000 feet, giving it seasonal weather with normal annual snowfall at over 100 inches. My overview of the six-year land-use conflict that occurred there is a summary of lived experience with dates and details confirmed by various sources (see Cole, "Snowbowl" and "Court"; Fischer, "Key Dates"; Muller, "Deadline" and "Draft"; and Tanner).

In October 2002, the United States Forest Service office in Flagstaff released a Proposed Action that invited public comments on the expansion of the Arizona Snowbowl, a ski resort located 14 miles from Flagstaff on the north side of the San Francisco Peaks. The Snowbowl resort leases 777 acres of Forest Service land, and the expansion, which included several more ski trails and a few more lifts, would remain within that acreage.

This proposal, however, was complicated by history, culture, and religion. Regional Native American tribes, including the Navajo and Hopi, consider the San Francisco Peaks sacred, a crucial spiritual location of the origin of life and where religious herbs and plants are found. Since 1938, when the Forest Service first built a road to the current location of the Snowbowl, the local tribes have protested each additional development on the Peaks. In 1979, contending that major development did not fit under the Forest Service's mandate to encourage mixed- and multiple-use on the public land, the tribes protested the plan to pave the road and build resort lodges. However, the litigation, which went to the Supreme Court, favored the Snowbowl owners. In the end, the court ruled that while the resort may *offend* religious practice, it did not *impede* it.

When the current owners of Snowbowl proposed the recent expansion, the key element of that expansion was the use of effluent, or treated wastewater. This water would be purchased from the city of Flagstaff and piped to the resort to enable snowmaking. Since 1999, Snowbowl has had inconsistent operations because of inconsistent snowfall resulting from a prolonged regional drought. In some of those years, the resort was open fewer than 21 days. The owners claim that snowmaking, a common practice for many ski resorts, is the only viable method to keep Snowbowl operating. Acknowledging the critical value of water in the high desert of Arizona, they proposed using effluent for that purpose, aware that effluent was already in use by the city to irrigate city property (including parks) and area golf courses.

In February 2004, per regulations for public land development, the U.S. Forest Service released the draft environmental impact statement (EIS) and opened it to public comments. In the EIS, which was written with the assistance of the consulting company SE Group, Inc., the U.S.F.S. outlined three options: 1) no change; 2) expansion of the resort with the use of reclaimed water for snowmaking; or 3) expansion of the resort without the use of snowmaking. The draft EIS nominally acknowledged the religious concerns of the Native American tribes without any discussion. The conclusion focused on the physical resources only: the effluent, with a Class A+ rating, would not harm the ecosystem or aquifer.

Water thus became the primary rhetorical and legal factor of this controversy. Opponents protested its use as desecration of a sacred mountain or as dangerous to the drinking water supply (openly questioning the no-harm claim). Proponents viewed effluent as a sustainable catalyst for increased tourism revenue spread throughout the city's businesses. The issue was argued about in letters to the editor, public forums, protests and debates at the local university, and city council meetings. The Chamber of Commerce lost members who opposed the Chamber's support of the resort. Other people were caught between their sympathy for indigenous rights and the prospect that their own ski recreation might cease.

Following the extended public comment period, the U.S.F.S. decided to proceed with the proposed expansion with the use of effluent for snowmaking in March 2005. In June of that year, the affected tribes, local and national organizations, and individuals filed separate lawsuits opposing the U.S.F.S. decision. The lawsuits were eventually combined, and in January 2006, a U.S. District judge sided with the U.S.F.S. In March 2007, a three-judge panel of the 9th Circuit Court of Appeals overruled the verdict in a preliminary ruling and sided with the tribes, but in August 2008, the full 9th Circuit Court of Appeals overturned that ruling, and Arizona Snowbowl began planning the infrastructure for snowmaking with reclaimed wastewater in 2009.

Values and Resource Terminology

While a seemingly nondescript physical resource, *water* was at the heart of the Snowbowl controversy; the language and rhetoric that arose from its physical properties ultimately defined and decided the issue in interesting ways. The underlying values and language of land use, resource use, and planning became the variables in how each side of the issue was perceived and judged. Stakeholders in this case study appropriated the authoritative and scientific influence of regulatory environmental and planning language for their own interests, introduced crude non-scientific terms, and often reduced the debate to mean-spirited statements that created a strong division among proponents and opponents.

The work of Alfred Guttenberg, a planning scholar who 40 years ago recognized that American planning is not "sufficiently conscious of its own language" (16), provides the basis for my exemplary framework of analysis of the Snowbowl situation. Guttenberg proposed a uniform standard of planning language in recognition of its influential role in "social evaluation and control":

> Not only is [planning] a form of social action, it is also action which achieves its effect through the use of signs and symbols. That is, land use planning is a language. Ordinarily, we do not think of planning as a language, and yet what else to planners use as tools of their trade if not words, mathematical notations, graphs, and lines on maps? These are all signs which are used either to represent existing reality or to give directions for changing that reality.[1] (50)

His proposed standard for planning language had two dimensions, and it is easy to find echoes of Aristotle's deliberative, forensic, and epideictic oratory. First, planning language can be classified according to what information it provides. Guttenberg describes three categories of this dimension: *referential* (what it is), *appraisive* (what its value or state is), and *prescriptive* (what it can be). The second dimension, tense, is an extension of the prescriptive classification: when prescribing change to something, the tense or mood of the phrasing influences the perception of the action. Those tenses are: *indicative* (is being, will be), *optative* (ought to be), *imperative* (must be, shall be), and *indeterminative* (perhaps can be, perhaps will be). The taxonomic potential of these dimensions is immense, but for composition students, I propose a modification of these two facets into one to make the analysis simpler without sacrificing adequate complexity. The *optative* tense in my modification retains its idealistic sense but focuses on how those ideals are put forward as a vocabulary of values. In this way, an optative value matches the definition of values put forward by Jonathan Turner and Charles Starnes, who state, "values are those highly general and abstract conceptions that provide the criteria for defining and assessing desirable conduct" (66). Because physical and social classifications in planning and land use terminology can't concretely account for cultural aspects that determine the very values that govern action, identifying values through discourse analysis uncovers different groups' conceptions of what *ought to be* and what is *desirable*—the underlying abstract elements. Therefore, I recommend placing the optative category along side the referential, appraisive, and prescriptive categories to create a simplified, one-dimensional classification of land-use and planning terms (see Table 1).

Referential	Appraisive	Prescriptive	Optative
What is	What worth or condition	What can be	What ought to be

Table 1: Modified-Guttenberg classification framework.

Introducing the *optative* category to textual analysis provides the means by which students can learn and identify societal values that are implicit in everyday behavior and rarely identified, examined, or critiqued by individuals. Furthermore, the additional category increases students' ability to make the discourse-ecology connections that are necessary for ecocomposition and sustainability-based curricula. Applied to planning language in documents such as environmental impact statements, the *optative* category makes clear the relationship, or lack of relationship, among the persistent values of modern society, which include the ideas of uninhibited progress and resource conservation. Depending on the interpretation, in other words, individuals' language will ascribe to the "American Dream" by *imperatively* growing a business, a household, or an institution. Or, someone might tout a conservationist attitude by buying a hybrid vehicle or installing solar cells on a house. Each of these actions is thus rhetorical: each is underscored by an ideal value or value system, which, if analyzed as part of the planning process, forces people—in often emotional ways—to prioritize constructed values in the support or opposition to proposed land-use projects.

Therefore, the modification and application of Guttenberg's planning categories here address two of Owens's tenets for integrating sustainability and composition. First, analyzing language of land-use conflicts provides "sustainability-conscious curricula" (27) and second, the implications of the *values* element analyzed through the optative category "would call attention to 'social traps' of unsustainability" where short-term effects are not in line with long-term, optative interests of global society (29). Furthermore, this method of analysis meets Dobrin's and Weisser's test for ecocomposition pedagogy—favoring a "discursive ecology" over a nature-writing curriculum. The modified-Guttenberg analysis allows students to navigate rhetorical complexities in land use through investigating non-literary discourse situated within a specific geographic, social, and cultural environment. By so doing, students engage in critical examination of the powerful social constructs that pervade society and thus create interesting contradictions among knowledge, values, behavior, and the environment.

The *optative* category's combination with Guttenberg's referential, appraisal, and prescriptive categories also allows analysis of "value" terms such as *sustainability* and *progress*. Relevant here is Michael Redclift's challenge of *sustainable development*, wherein he critiques the phrase's inherent assumption of continuous scientific progress:

> By incorporating the concept of "sustainability" within the account of "development," the discourse surrounding the environment is often used to strengthen, rather than weaken, the basic supposition about progress. *Development is read as synonymous with progress, and made more palatable because it is linked with "natural" limits, expressed in the concept of sustainability.* (7, emphasis added)

The *progress* value, defined by Turner and Starnes, is present in efforts to "control the world and achieve material comfort" that "cumulatively . . . allow both the individual and society to progress to a higher level than previously possible" (70). As a "desirable" end, progress is firmly aligned with the American concept of *success*, which, as a factor for social mobility, can be as powerful and motivating as religion governing action (Lipset 529). For many, achievement and success are unabashedly pursued without ecological consideration, supported by the *individualist, nationalist,* and *efficient/produc-tive* American values (Sliwiak and Fissell 159). Thus, Redclift's recognition that sustainability's emergence is nonetheless attached to, even subverted by, progress illustrates the importance of educational exercises that further a "clarification of values" (see Clark, Heinberg).

Relevant to the Snowbowl case study would be an analysis of the value systems of the Native Americans in contrast to the prevailing values of Americans of European descent. Such an initial clarification is not actually necessary because the analysis of language and rhetoric with the modified-Guttenberg framework, as I show later, explicitly illustrates the differences in values. But for students, allowing them to speculate values before analyzing the language of the stakeholders, even if stereotypical, would compound the impact that the analysis later reveals. In my own case, I find that Native American values are often idealized by writers, and as a collective group, their cultural values are portrayed as starkly different from Western mainstream society in terms of progress and humans' relationship to the land. Writers such as Wendell Berry have made distinctions between the European/American inclination to exploit land and the Native American proclivity for nurturing land (7). Annie Booth and Harvey Jacobs note that Native Americans do not view any "emptiness in the world" because nature was full of life already (32) and thus any "progress" for humanity is always achieved at the cost of life. Rather than ascribing to scientific methodology or categorization, "Native Americans imagine themselves specifically in terms of relationships with the physical world, among *other* things" (Booth and Jacobs 39, emphasis added). The veneration of Native American values can be inspiring, but like any idealized notion about specific cultures, acquaintance with individuals from those cultures can raise doubts about the extent such values permeate. For example, setting up cultures as examples for appropriate environmental behavior, as has happened with Native Americans, ignores the inconsistencies in members of those cultures consciously buying and using "progressing" American products that exist from "exploitation" of natural resources.

For a time, I wondered if Native Americans and their idealized views were being exploited by people opposed to the Snowbowl expansion, as many of the Native Americans (mostly students) I knew didn't have strong opinions initially. Furthermore, because of the legal precedents in the lease agreement, it seemed as if the Snowbowl were not obligated to argue the issue of "sacredness" again. And the unappealing imagery of the rhetoric used in opposition to the reclaimed water—evoking large amounts of "poop" and "pee" pumped onto the mountain—seemed to misrepresent the scientific analysis of the quality of the treated water for non-potable use, which degraded the debate. But the discourse analysis employed here quickly clarified the underlying value structures of the stakeholders and illustrates that one's position on the conflict can be clarified by dissecting and classifying language.

Conflict-Language Analysis

In addition to his two-dimensional standard planning language proposal, Guttenberg also produced a rhetorical model that typifies the land-use conflicts that result from planning language ambiguity. First, Guttenberg posits, involved parties (planners, developers, opponents) devise communication in order to arouse and organize public sentiment on their behalf. Since the initial stakeholders constitute only a portion of the total population, this communication will attempt to secure general agreement that a central resource or planning term is good or bad. This means placing the term in a context in which it appears to support or contradict specific, constructed values of society. Second, the stakeholders characterize the term mundanely so as to appeal to the real as well as the ideal motives of the general community. The third part of Guttenberg's model suggests that parties communicate to the public how the term might also threaten one personally (9). Guttenberg's model of the manipulation of planning language illustrates his recognition of how intentional, persuasive use of context and terminology can and will influence malleable audiences.

Consequently, an important step in the more involved *conflict-language analysis* is a basic *term analysis*. For any land-use conflict, students can be directed to identify the central planning or resource term that is manipulated by different sides. For example, Table 2 illustrates the application of Guttenberg's model to the Snowbowl conflict, showing how stakeholding proponents and opponents of the snowmaking plan utilized language to appeal to the public and courts. Interestingly, *reclaimed water*, not *effluent*, was how the planners chose to refer to it generally, and that became the common term in the media perhaps because of its mundane qualities.

While there are several valuable exercises and arguments that instructors and students can devise from *term analysis*, further close analysis using the modified-Guttenberg classification system clarifies the way that manipulated language both informs and is informed by a language, rhetoric, and terminology of values. Conflict-language analysis of collected documents adds a more thorough taxonomy of the various stakeholders' language. For the most part, the Executive Summary of environmental impact statements will provide sufficient language to classify the terms, but additional sections and documents might be necessary to more fully understand the values of the planning/developing entities. Other necessary sources include community newspapers, university research, and websites of opposition groups, businesses, planning consultants, and government institutions.

In the classroom, both term analysis and conflict-language analysis can be conducted at any point in the development of a land-use conflict. While there are obvious advantages, especially for *situated practice*, for students becoming involved early, these cases last much longer than a semester, which would have to be considered. For my example, I began this analysis following early court decisions, using material covering the entire six-year process—from the draft EIS to the 9th Circuit Court's opinion. The remainder of this section consists of selected quotes from the various stakeholders involved in the San Francisco Peaks conflict, followed by a classification of the language into categories: 1) referential; 2) appraisive; 3) prescriptive; and 4) optative. Each classification is accompanied by brief comments analyzing how the classification indicates values of the stakeholders.

Guttenberg's model	Proponents	Opponents
1. Make term (*effluent*) bad/good	• Used *Reclaimed water;* not • *Treated sewage, Treated wastewater,* or *Effluent*	• Used *Pee, Poop,* or *Sewage;* chose not to use *Reclaimed water* as often as proponents.
2. Characterize *effluent* as mundane and real	• Reclaimed water for snowmaking puts water back into the aquifer and saves regular water.	• Reclaimed water is a waste of water and is expensive
3. Show how *effluent* hurts/helps you or specific people	• Reclaimed water allows Snowbowl to stay open, keeping tourist dollars in Flagstaff	• Reclaimed water does not respect the sacredness of the Peaks to Native Americans and has hidden toxins that would harm people.

Table 2: Term analysis of opponents' and proponents' use of effluent.

Stakeholder: U.S. Forest Service

From the executive summary of *Final Environmental Impact Statement (FEIS)*:

> The Forest Service and Snowbowl cooperatively determined general categories important for improving the Snowbowl's facilities. From these categories, a list of proposed projects was created, and the Proposed Action ultimately emerged. The overall Purpose and Need for these projects responds to two broad categories: 1) to provide a consistent/reliable operating season, and 2) to improve safety, skiing conditions, and recreational opportunities by bringing terrain and infrastructure into balance with existing demand. . . .

> The two issues that emerged from the scoping process were related to heritage resources. These issues warranted the creation of an additional alternative." . . .[Those issues were that] 1) "the use of reclaimed wastewater

as a water source may impact cultural and spiritual values associated with the San Francisco Peaks;" . . . and 2) "proposed ground disturbances and vegetation removal may result in permanently evident, visible alterations (e.g. "scarring") of the San Francisco Peaks.

Referential	Appraisive	Prescriptive	Optative
• Snowbowl's facilities • "Hertitage resources" • Cooperative project between USFS and Snowbowl	• Needs improving • Inconsistent/ Unreliable operating season • Terrain and infrastructure are not in balance with demand • "Heritage" must be considered but does not trump economic concerns	• Make snow with reclaimed water • Upgrade lifts • Add terrain • Build parking lot, access road	• Safety • Recreational opportunities • Consistency • Economic gain • "Scarring" may occur

Table 3: Classification of Forest Service statement.

The U.S.F.S. is the governing organization of the land in question, both as a government institution charged with its care, and also as the "owner" of the land with the ability to lease the land for the use of the Arizona Snowbowl. The U.S.F.S. was also the primary planning entity, assisted by the SE Group, a planning firm specializing in ski resort development. The language of the EIS quoted above clearly reflects the values and interests of the leasee of the land, with the Purpose and Need aimed directly at the highly-prized values of safety, progress, efficiency/productivity, and leisure tourism. Yet significantly, the "scoping process" mentioned took place only two months before the draft EIS was released to the public, and the "alternative option" based on the issues raised by that scoping did not appear until the Final EIS. The lateness of the scoping of tribal concerns, along with the diversion of their concerns to alternative status in the EIS, indicate further that the underlying values of the Native Americans were, understandably, less important than the initial optative language put forward by the planners.

Stakeholder: Arizona Snowbowl

From Snowbowl personnel (quotes from local newspaper and website):

The resort, one of two in the state, might go out of business because of a lack of consistent snowfall. The plans won't expand the footprint of the ski area, which occupies less than 1 percent of the Peaks. (Kravets)

Snowbowl is located on already-disturbed public land, that reclaimed water has been deemed environmentally safe for snowmaking and the Supreme Court has previously held that a group's religious or spiritual beliefs can't prohibit mixed uses of public lands as long as the beliefs can be accommodated. (Kravets)

Referential	Appraisive	Prescriptive	Optative
• Snowbowl • The Peaks • The resort • Public land	• Public land is already disturbed • Reclaimed water is environmentally safe • The resort is financially teetering • Resort and expansion is less than 1% of Peaks	• Beliefs can be accommodated under Proposed Action because footprint is the same and water is safe	• Business interests are important • Supreme Court decision is unquestionable

Table 5: Classification of Snowbowl personnel language.

The Arizona Snowbowl prioritizes the economic "need" and importance of the ski resort, raising the possibility of "going out of business," which appeals to distinct recessionary fears that contradict the inevitability of progress. The majority of the language quoted above nominally acknowledging the concerns of the opponents, and treats lightly those concerns by the using "accommodate beliefs" in the same sentence as "already-disturbed land." The additional appeal to the authority of Supreme Court, along with the mention of the small footprint of the proposed action, appeal to typical American values, but these can contrast with Native American ideas of fairness and a holistic land ethic.

Stakeholder: Save the Peaks Coalition

From Save the Peaks website:
- To protect spiritual and cultural rights
- To foster mutual respect among all people and ensure a high quality of life for all peoples potentially affected.
- To conserve water for the future, when true needs will be greater, and the drought perhaps more severe.
- To prevent habitat disruption and fragmentation, and other threats to endangered plants and animals.
- To defend Flagstaff from Ski Town Syndrome. We may not become Vail or Aspen, but what will we become if we value things like increased

skiing more highly than the Peaks' exceptional beauty, habitat and cultural importance? ("About Us")

Referential	Appraisive	Prescriptive	Optative
• Flagstaff • Peaks	• Need for water not great • Plants and animals in danger	• Protect spiritual and cultural rights • Conserve water • Prevent habitat disruption • Defend against Ski Town Syndrome	• Religious freedom and cultural awareness • Quality of life for everyone • Beauty, culture valued above skiing

Table 6: Classification of Save the Peaks Coalition goals.

The Save the Peaks Coalition, describing itself as "a group of concerned citizens, agencies, business people, religious and spiritual leaders, skiers, snowboarders, conservationists, students, teachers and taxpayers" ("About Us"), opposed the initial Proposed Action and continue to advocate for continued care for cultural and land preservation. Analyzing a sample of the Coalition's objectives, the group clearly takes a broad view of the situation. Their opposition to snowmaking is portrayed as a part of their wider platform: to promote the respect of religion, cultures, and all forms of life. Expanding the issue in this way frames the conflict around optative values, as indicated by Table 6 above. The mountain and its inhabitants and "clients" represent more, in this rhetoric, than economic partners in the growth and viability of a business interest. Comparing the values in the optative language of the Coalition with the values represented by the Snowbowl in their optative column, the Coalition's values are universally appealing but not necessarily more prized than the job-creation, tourism-dollar, economic justifications for keeping the Snowbowl consistent.

Stakeholders: Native American Tribe Members

Tribal member perspectives:

> It is up to the deities, not man, to make snow. To usurp their authority is a crime, an insult. It desecrates the entire mountain that the Hopi believe is a living entity. (Kravets)

> Allowing snow made with reclaimed wastewater and spread on the San Francisco Peaks [is like] a child watching his or her mother being raped. (Cole, "Shirley")

Spraying snow made from treated sewage on the Peaks is like putting a contaminated needle in your body containing poison. (Kravets)

Referential	Appraisive	Prescriptive	Optative
• San Francisco Peaks • Entire mountain	•Treated sewage • Reclaimed wastewater • Desecration	• Leave mountain alone • Let nature/gods make snow	• Mountain is a living entity • Usurping authority of deities is wrong • Snowmaking = Rape = Poisoning

Table 7: Classification of Tribal member quotes.

The statements from tribal members above reflect a deeper feeling about the use of land than most European-descended whites understand, which perhaps led to many non-Native Americans scoffing at such strong comparisons of "rape" or "poisoning" to snowmaking. The local newspaper in Flagstaff stated that according to court testimony, tribal members additionally blamed misuse of the Peaks for the World Trade Center attacks, the Columbia space shuttle crash, and natural disasters (Cole, "Culture Clash"). For people who believe in a generational and ecological connection to a divine, living landscape, such connections make sense, while those holding more empirical, scientific traditions have difficulty linking seemingly unrelated events. This cultural gap emerges from a relationship with the land for generations:

> Native Americans have been determining themselves in their imagination for many generations, and in the process, the landscape has become part of the particular reality. In a sense, for the Native American, the process is more intuitive and evolutionary than is the white Western rational linear process. (Booth and Jacobs 39)

Such descriptions of Native American perspectives, along with the extraordinary connections made by members of that culture, confirm the "wicked" nature of this conflict. A planning entity within an American society that values science, efficiency and professionalism will struggle to resolve values-laden situations when interested parties paradoxically value generational and mystical connections between humans and the landscape, which do not require expertise or machinery to understand.

The Court Decisions

From the sustainability perspective, the Snowbowl's snowmaking proposal does indeed spare aquifer water in order to sustain a more consistent ski season, benefiting the owners, employees, skiers, and the businesses of Flagstaff. The plan's sustainability was a means to adhere to the progress value, especially the inevitability of it, while fitting within the prevailing water issues of the area. Progress was prioritized for reasons of viability—the owners were likely sincere in having to close Snowbowl without snowmaking—yet that overshadowed an earnest assessment of other cultural effects. With water as the catalyst for economic sustainability for the Snowbowl owners, the opponents of the snowmaking proposal used water to protest and battle within the constraints of environmental and religious legal precedent. The larger issue, evident in their formal and informal discourse sampled above, was their holistic view of the relationship between humans and land, but the narrow legal definitions of religious practice—one can offend but cannot impede—precluded the focus on the non-purity of the effluent.

Therefore, while the U.S. District judge, who first heard the case, found that the opponents of the Snowbowl "failed to present any objective evidence that their exercise of religion will be impacted by the Snowbowl upgrades" (Kravets), the pure-water aspect apparently was convincing to the preliminary panel of the 9th Circuit Court of Appeals. Since water from the Peaks is used in religious ceremonies, the panel wrote that any purposeful tainting of the water would infringe on religious practice. Furthermore, using a strong metaphor, the panel compares using snowmelt that contains reclaimed water to requiring baptisms to be done in reclaimed water. Interestingly, while the decision of the judges reflects sympathy for the beliefs of the Native Americans, the choice of metaphor repeats the situated vocabulary of the District Court by couching Native American religious philosophy within a Western traditional religious practice or exercise. Historically, people have been baptized in less appealing water than purified wastewater, and the religious practices of the Native Americans are actually not impeded by a touch of chemical in snowmelt. The pure water aspect of the conflict was successful in court only because the Native American belief in everything as a living part of a whole would not be, for that belief is inarticulate with the pervasive persistence of economic progression in our society. But infringement on water-based religious activities can be measured and thus became the central tactic for the opponents. The recognition of these uses of language is at the heart of this method of analysis, confirming Abbey's intimation that changes in vocabularies of values create actual results.

However, the panel's interpretation in regard to the water differed from the full Circuit Court majority opinion reversal. The reversed ruling states that "snowmaking with water containing 0.0001 percent human waste does not run afoul of the federal Religious Freedom Restoration Act because it doesn't go far enough to meet the legal test of violating religious freedom," which is tested by "whether a government action forces a person to violate their own religious beliefs" ("Court"). The dissenting minority of the court stated that the ruling "misunderstands the very nature of religion" ("Court"), recognizing the difference in religious philosophy and practice. The majority decision, however, draws the line between "personalized oversight" and established means of public deliberation and comment:

> [If this case met the test for violating religious freedom], any action the federal government were to take, including action on its own land, would be subject to the personalized oversight of millions of citizens. Each citizen would hold an individual veto to prohibit the government action solely because it offends his religious beliefs, sensibilities, or tastes, or fails to satisfy his religious desires. Further, giving one religious sect a veto over the use of public park land would deprive others of the right to use what is, by definition, land that belongs to everyone. ("Court")

The 9th Circuit Court effectively endorses the established means for conducting government planning and resolving conflicts. By emphasizing the singular individual, which, it should be noted, was not the tribes' situation, the Court seemed to balance the majority rights of public land with the ideals of numerous potential cultural minorities. The "government" here represents the citizens of the nation, and thus institutional and professional methods and procedures are, according to the Court, the best method for making decision for "its own land" that "belongs to everyone."

Yet such a position can be frustrating to individuals representing the "growing pluralism of contemporary publics, whose valuation of proposals are judged against an array of different and contradicting scales" (Rittel and Webber 167). Further, "the classical paradigm of science and engineering—the paradigm that has underlain modern professionalism—is not applicable to the problems of open societal systems" (160). In our deference to organizational oversight, as Craig Waddell notes, "the public is still obliged to endure the effects of economic and environmental decisions upon which it has little or no influence—decisions that are left, instead, to experts in science, industry and government" (202). Decades of industrialization and mainstream progress affect the public's acceptance of certain vocabulary of values emanating from professionals and experts, meaning that job *creation*, economic *health*, and *thriving* local businesses, for example, outweigh vocabularies that are less in line with supercultural values of economic growth and progress. A Hopi medicine man, a plaintiff in the lawsuit, had his cynical theory: "It's never going to go our way, no matter what kind of government it is, when there's money involved" ("Court").

Conclusion

The *term analysis* and *conflict-language analysis* conducted in this article are examples of how a sustainability-conscious curriculum can utilize values clarification to understand ecological discourse. The modified-Guttenberg framework deconstructs the language and rhetoric to accentuate the differences among the values of the stakeholders, not to mention the values of the students analyzing the conflict. As Guttenberg suggests, in traditional, referential planning language, many cultural and landscape factors are ignored. Values analysis of the language can lead to a better understanding of what those factors are and why they are not considered. The statements made by the Native Americans in this case study are grounded in a local but deep cultural affinity, and thus explicitly use optative-value language to refer to localized land quality and prescriptive use of what is familiar. The U.S.F.S. language and the Snowbowl's messages, by contrast, comprise a larger cultural affinity to progress, and thus reflect traditional, land-management referential and appraisive language that encourages imperative or indicative prescriptions for land-use situations. The breaking down of the language above illustrates that each of the optative classifications is in some sense valued by most members of society. The conflict analysis exposes the difficulty of concrete decisions based on those easily manipulated abstract values.

Therefore, the modified-Guttenberg framework used here can show how vocabularies of values can reflect or not reflect an attitude of inclusion, where non-economic factors such as belief systems are given equal consideration to progressive factors when evaluating environmental impact (see Peterson and Peterson). According to Redclift, moving beyond a strictly progressive paradigm requires us to "explore the need to change our underlying social commitments" (19). The analysis employed here reveals cultural nuances that clarify the values that in many cases determine those commitments. By highlighting specific, competing social values in complex land-use conflicts, conducting a "discursive ecology" analysis in a composition course illustrates that values and their vocabulary can be examined, critiqued, and utilized for long-term foresight. Doing so would provide a fuller understanding of "wicked problems" so that cultural and other variables are as equally considered in resolutions as economic and narrowly defined environmental effects. By facilitating the recognition of values through the examination of how vocabulary carries those values, our field can broaden the optative sensibilities of our students and meaningfully contribute to the critical issues of planning and sustainability.

Notes

1. Guttenberg's sense of land use planning's influence on social reality and living patterns reflects what Harvey calls the "immobility" of "fixed capital in the built environment," causing people to commit "to certain patterns of use for an extended time within the particularity of spatial location" (83).

Works Cited

Abbey, Edward. *A Voice Crying in the Wilderness*. New York: St. Martin's, 1989. Print.

About Us. Save the Peaks Coalition. Web. 15 Oct. 2007.

Allen, Patricia L. and Carolyn E. Sachs. "The Social Side of Sustainability: Class, Gender, and Race." *Science as Culture* (1991): 569-90. Print.

Berry, Wendell. *The Unsettling of America*. 1977. San Francisco: Sierra Club Books, 1996. Print.

Booth, Annie L., and Harvey M. Jacobs. "Ties That Bind: Native American Beliefs as a Foundation for Environmental Consciousness." *Environmental Ethics* 12 (1990): 27-43. Print.

Braun, Annie. "Hundreds to March For Sacred Sites." *Arizona Daily Sun* 25 Mar. 2006. Web. 02 Oct. 2007.

Clark, Mary E. "Changes in Euro-American Values Needed for Sustainability." *Journal of Social Issues* 51.4 (1995): 63-82. Print.

Cole, Cyndy. "Shirley: Navajo Religious Freedom at Stake." *Arizona Daily Sun* 3 Nov. 2005. Web. 02 Oct. 2007.

———. "Snowbowl: Culture Clash." *Arizona Daily Sun* 14 Nov. 2006. Web. 02 Oct. 2007.

———. "Snowbowl Owner Vows to Pursue Snowmaking." *Arizona Daily Sun* 13 Mar. 2007. Web. 02 Oct. 2007.

Cope, Bill, and Mary Kalantzis, eds. *Multiliteracies: Literacy Learning and the Design of Social Futures*. New York: Routledge, 2000. Print.

Dobrin, Sidney, and Christian Weisser. *Natural Discourse: Toward Ecocomposition*. Albany: SUNY P, 2002. Print.

Fischer, Howard. "Snowbowl Fight Rages On." *Arizona Daily Sun* 13 Mar. 2007. Web. 02 Oct. 2007.

Goggin, Peter and Zach Waggoner. "Sustainable Development: Thinking Globally and Acting Locally in the Writing Classroom." *Composition Studies* 33.2 (2005): 45-67. Print.

Guttenberg, Albert Z. *The Language of Planning*. Urbana: U of Illinois P, 1993. Print.

Harvey, David. *Spaces of Capital: Towards a Critical Geography*. New York: Routledge, 2001. Print.

Hawisher, Gail E., Paul LeBlanc, Charles Moran, Cynthia L. Selfe. *Computers and the Teaching of Writing in American Higher Education, 1979-1994: A History*. Norwood: Ablex, 1996. Print.

Heinberg, Richard. "Toward a New Definition of Progress." *Futurist* Jul. 1997: 60. Print.

In the News. Arizona Snowbowl Press Releases. Web. 10 Oct. 2007.

"Key Dates in Arizona Snowbowl History." *Arizona Daily Sun* 13 Mar. 2007. Web. 02 Oct. 2007.

Kravets, David. "Indians Say Arizona Ski Resort Desecrates Their Sacred Mountains. *Santa Fe New Mexican* 12 Sep. 2006. Web. 02 Oct. 2007.

Lipset, Seymour, M. "The Value Patterns of Democracy: A Case Study in Comparative Analysis." *American Sociological Review* (1963-64): 515-31. Print.

Muller, Seth. "Deadline Looms for Comment on Snowbowl Upgrade Plan." *Arizona Daily Sun* 13 Apr. 2004. Web. 02 Oct. 2007.

———. "Draft Snowmaking Plan Draws Hundreds." *Arizona Daily Sun* 26 Feb. 2004. Web. 02 Oct. 2007.

Owens, Derek. *Composition and Sustainability: Teaching for a Threatened Generation*. Urbana: NCTE, 2001. Print.

Peterson, Markus J., and Tarla Rai Peterson. "A Rhetorical Critique of 'Nonmarket' Economic Valuations for Natural Resources." *Environmental Values* 2 (1993): 47-65. Print.

Redclift, Michael. "Sustainable Development: Needs, Values, Rights." *Environmental Values* 2 (1993): 3-20. Print.

Rittel, Horst W. J., and Melvin M. Webber. "Dilemmas in a General Theory of Planning." *Policy Sciences* 4 (1973): 155-69. Print.

Sliwiak, Stanley A., and Susan Frissell. "Some Value Orientations and Their Educational Implications in American Society." *Education* 108.2 (1987): 153. Print.

Staff and Capitol Media Services. "Court: Arizona Snowbowl Can Make Snow With Reclaimed Wastewater." *Arizona Daily Sun* 08 Aug. 2008. Web. 09 Nov. 2008.

Tanner, Adam. "U.S. Court Backs Indian Tribe on Sacred Mountain. *San Diego Union-Tribune* 12 Mar. 2007. Web. 02 Oct. 2007.

Turner, Jonathan H., and Charles E. Starnes. *Inequality: Privilege and Poverty in America*. San Francisco: Pacific Publishers, 1976. Print.

United States Forest Service. *Final Environmental Impact Statement, Vol. 1*. 2005. Web. 02 Sep. 2007.

Waddell, Craig. "Defining Sustainable Development: A Case Study in Environmental Communication." *Technical Communication Quarterly,* 4.2 (1995): 201-16. Print.

"I Hope It's Just Attendance": What Does Participation Mean to Freshman Composition Students and Instructors?

Kerry Dirk

Participation, a commonly graded component of composition classrooms, is rarely the focus of current research studies. While some discussions have addressed grading practices or ways to increase participation, student and instructor voices have yet to be included in studies of classroom participation in composition courses. Yet these voices are necessary to discover how students and instructors define participation, as well as to determine their beliefs about, and justifications for, grading this activity. There is reason to suppose that students and instructors often have disparate ideas about what constitutes composition classroom participation. When asked why he or she grades participation, one instructor explained:

> Participation is extremely important. The students are not passive vessels in which I pour information. I tell them that they are the best teachers they will ever have. But, to teach themselves they need to question, discuss, share their ideas and insights with others. They learn from each other. Without participation we might as well plop them down in front of a computer or television and have them watch. They learn by doing, by writing.

It would be difficult to disagree with this instructor's justification for choosing to include participation as a requirement for the course. Yet the responses from the students in the study that follows suggest that they place less value on this part of the course. One student wrote, "As long as you don't fall asleep, you will be alright." As this response reveals, there seems to be a wide discrepancy between instructor and student beliefs about what qualifies as participation in the classroom. The findings that I report in the remainder of this article reveal not only troubling definitions of participation but also nebulous grading practices of this classroom component.

Review of Literature

The composition classroom is often thought to be a prime location for fostering critical thinking skills and creating active learners. Since process pedagogy's rise in the 1970s, many composition classes continue to utilize activities that developed out of this movement, such as workshops, revision strategies, free writing, class discussion, and group work (Tobin). Many of us would agree with Peter Elbow's belief that "writing is a way to end up thinking something you couldn't have started out thinking" (*Writing* 15) or with Donald Murray's assertion that "we certainly should allow time within the curriculum for prewriting, and we should work with our students to help them understand the process of rehearsal, to allow them the experience of rehearsing what they will write in their minds, on the paper, and with collaborators" (380-81). Scholars such as Kenneth Bruffee and John Trimbur have also argued convincingly that the exchange of ideas within the classroom is essential to student learning. While Bruffee argues that "writing always has its roots deep in the acquired ability to carry on the social symbolic exchange we call conversation" (641-42) and understands the goal of collaborative learning to be consensus among students, Trimbur claims that he is "less interested in students achieving consensus (although of course this happens at times) as in their using consensus as a critical instrument to open gaps in the conversation through which differences may emerge" (614). Consensus or not, classroom discussion, along with these other in-class activities, has become an integral part of the writing classroom.

It would be beyond the scope of this paper to trace the development of these activities in the contemporary classroom. More recently, however, John Bean's *Engaging Ideas* has provided instructors with detailed writing activities for all disciplines. He explains that the premise of his book is "that integrating writing and other critical thinking activities into a course increases students' learning while teaching them thinking skills for posing questions, proposing hypotheses, gathering and analyzing data, and making arguments" (1). Many of Bean's activities make use of collaborative methods, and he additionally includes activities that center on group work, revision, journals, and portfolios—all of which stem from process pedagogy.

To make students accountable for these classroom activities, composition instructors often include classroom involvement as participation and include participation within the overall course grade. Email responses from a listserv of freshman composition instructors, as well as an email to writing instructors in my department, confirmed that this criterion is standard in freshman composition as well and that it accounted for an average of 15% of a student's grade.[1] Bean and Peterson argue that "grading class participation can send positive signals to students about the kind of learning and thinking an instructor values, such as growth in critical thinking, active learning, development of listening and speaking skills needed for career success, and the ability to join a discipline's conversation" (33). Clearly, these outcomes are desirable, making the inclusion of a participation grade seem to be a logical choice among instructors.

Composition class aside, participation seems to be most often defined as verbal contributions to class, including asking and answering questions and participating in class discussions. Indeed, most scholars who have conducted studies of student participation have approached the concept of participation with this definition (Auster and MacRone; Crombie et al; Fassinger; Nunn; Ryan, Marshall, and Haomiao). As a result, these studies have focused on issues rooted in class discussions, such as the effects of instructor and student genders and students' perceptions of their level of contribution.

The only study that has specifically focused on definitions of participation was conducted by Linda Fritschner, who found that quiet and talkative students define participation in two very different ways: "'Talkers,' those students who made two or more comments per class, tended to define participation as simply 'voluntarily speaking out in class.' Quiet students defined participation as . . . attendance, active listening, sitting in their seats, doing the assignments, and being prepared for class" (352). Further, she found that instructors most commonly grouped participation into one of six levels. [2] Surprisingly, students in Fritschner's study seemed to define participation at levels higher on Fritschner's scale than most surveyed instructors, many of whom felt they had too much information to present, leaving no time for much beyond lecture.

However, unlike instructors of lecture-based classrooms, most composition instructors expect students to participate at high levels, as student involvement often comprises the core of the writing classroom experience. Bean and Peterson hope that "when students see that their participation is being graded regularly and consistently, they adjust their study habits accordingly to be prepared for active participation" (33). Unfortunately, despite their being graded for participation, students often choose not to participate as much as instructors would like. A recent survey, which focused on students' first college year, found that freshman had a lack of interest in academic study, choosing instead to focus their attention on social activities such as texting or blogging (Bauerlein). These results are problematic, as the connection between student engagement and the improved development of critical thinking skills has long been established (Halpern; McKeachie; Smith; Tsui).

A recent study of the relation between critical thinking and academic control among first year students found that students who feel more in control of their academic experience are more likely to engage in critical thinking and to have improved learning experience (Stupnisky, et al.).[3] Citing previous studies by Perry, which link perceived academic control to academic success, the researchers argue that students in college are often in situations over which they feel little control. As a result, Stupnisky et al. posit: "students who believe they can influence their academic outcomes (i.e., high perceived control) should be more willing to put forth the effort to think critically (i.e., high critical thinking)" (517). Consequently, they recommend that to increase students' disposition to think critically, instructors should create a high-control environment by providing detailed assignments, study suggestions, instructor availability, etc. Furthermore, students should have a clear understanding of how to succeed, as Stupnisky et al. found that "students who felt more in control of their academic outcomes at the start of the academic year were more likely to think critically later in the year" (524). However, if instructors have unclear participation expectations and are using ambiguous grading practices, then it would not be surprising to find that students believe they have little control over their participation grade, possibly creating further disengagement and a decreased inclination to develop critical thinking skills.

These previous studies, which mostly assume the definition of participation to be discussion, limit the chance to study the wide variations of definitions of participation that may be used in composition classrooms, in particular. No research on the meaning of participation within the composition classroom has been done, and no research has compared student and instructor definitions to see if discrepancies occur. Additionally, despite the fact that most instructors choose to include participation in their overall course grade, no studies in composition have surveyed instructors about their use of this grading practice. To discover whether students are indeed aware of their instructors' expectations for participation, and to learn how instructors grade participation, I conducted the following study. If students are being graded for participation (and many are), then it is important that they understand what is required of them in order to receive full credit, as this greater control over their grades may also further the development of their critical thinking skills through their engagement in classroom activities.

The purpose of this study was to determine how students define participation within the composition classroom and to compare that definition to their instructors', as well as to the definitions of students taking different sections of the same course. It was also designed to determine how instructors grade participation and why. The study was designed to consider the following questions:

1. How much is participation worth in most composition classes? Are students aware of this percentage?
2. How do instructors define participation?
3. How do instructors grade participation?
4. How do students define participation?
5. What do students believe is most important for them to earn their participation grade?
6. How do students believe their instructors will grade participation?
7. Why do instructors choose to include participation as a part of their course grade?

Methodology

Participants

The participants in this study included 20 freshman composition instructors and 344 students enrolled in freshman composition courses at a medium-sized, public, doctoral-granting institution located in the Midwest. Freshman composition courses at this university are taught primarily by graduate students, although adjunct and full-time faculty teach several sections each quarter. While there is some variety in materials used for these courses, all freshman composition courses share four common goals for students: reading rhetorically, researching rhetorically, writing rhetorically, and responding rhetorically. Instructors are permitted to create their own syllabi for these courses and to determine their own grading criteria.

In order to select participants, I identified and emailed each instructor of freshman composition for Winter Quarter of 2007. Of the 50 instructors who were emailed, 20 agreed to let me visit their class and to give students my survey. These instructors also agreed to fill out a survey designed for them.

Materials

With the help of other experienced instructors of composition, I designed two surveys to be used in this study (See Appendices A & B). The survey intended for the students included questions concerning their definitions of participation in their composition courses, and the survey for the instructors included questions concerning their definitions of participation for these courses. The questions were purposely made open-ended to allow for a greater variety of responses.

Procedure

This study was conducted during weeks seven through ten of a ten-week quarter to assure that students had ample time to become familiar with their classes. I visited each of the twenty classes sometime during its regularly scheduled meeting, at which time I passed out the surveys. I briefly explained the nature of the study, and students were given as much time as needed to complete the surveys. This process took ten to twenty minutes. I collected the surveys from students as they completed them. I also handed out instructor surveys at this time, although instructors were permitted to complete them on their own time and to put them in my departmental mailbox.

Analysis

In order to study the data carefully, I began by identifying and tallying the various responses for each class. I noticed that students' definitions of participation were similar despite the open-ended questions on the survey, making it easier than expected to combine the data. For example, I counted how many students mentioned activities such as attendance, discussion, and peer review under the question that asked them what their instructor counts as participation. Further, I counted two seemingly identical yet differently named activities as one activity; for example, I grouped "paying attention" and "listening" into the same category, as well as "free writes" and "in-class writing." I also chose not to group together activities that many instructors might have counted as the same. For example, "asking questions" and "answering questions" could be seen as inclusive of class discussion, but both instructors and students most often listed these in addition to class discussion.

After completing this process for each class, I added the data from the classes together. I decided to focus on four things:

1. The students' understanding of how much attendance is worth.
2. The students' explanation of what they believe counts toward their participation grade.
3. The students' ranking of the top four activities they must do to earn their participation grade.
4. The students' understanding of how their instructors grade their participation.

I approached the instructors' data in the same manner and also found many similarities in responses. To correspond to the student data, I decided to focus on the following:

1. The percentage of the grades which instructors make participation worth.
2. The top four activities instructors count as part of the participation grade.
3. The instructors' explanations of how they grade participation.
4. The reasons why instructors choose to grade participation.

This method of analysis allowed me to compare student responses, instructor responses, and student-instructor responses.

Student Results

In these twenty classes, participation ranged from 0-20% of the students' grade (See Table 1). Four of the instructors did not include participation as a part of their core course grade; participation was not graded at all in two of the classes, and in the other two courses, it could only positively affect a student's grade as extra credit. In general, the participation grade was significant enough to affect the overall class grade. One might suppose that students would want to succeed in class and would show awareness of how much participation might affect their final grade. However, only 90 out of 344 (26.2%) of the students who answered this question knew how much participation was worth as a part of their course grade.

Number of Instructors	Percent of Grade Participation is Worth
4	0%
2	5%
1	8%
5	10%
3	15%
5	20%

Table 1. Participation Grade Percentages

When students were asked to list everything that they believe their instructor counts toward their participation grade, students most often listed class discussions (77.0%), attendance (34.4%), homework (28.8%), and in-class writing (20.3%)(See Table 2).

Activity	Number of students out of 344 who included this activity	Percentage of students who included this activity
Class Discussion	265	77.0%
Attendance	118	34.3%
Homework	99	28.8%
In-class Writing	70	20.3%
Answer Questions	68	19.8%
Group work	49	14.2%
Pay attention	36	10.5%
Ask questions	36	10.5%
Peer Review	30	8.7%
Journal	25	7.3%
Other	25	7.3%
Read aloud	25	7.3%
Voice Opinion	21	6.1%

Table 2. Activities Students Believe Count for Participation

Students were also asked to rank the top four things they believed they had to do to earn their participation grade. While the activities listed were very diverse, including reading, group work, peer review, being polite, and thinking, among others, there were also several activities that were repeatedly ranked in the top four. Of the 334 students who listed a top activity,

35.9% listed class discussion, 28.7% listed attendance, 11.4% listed homework, and 6.0% listed answering questions. For the second most important activity which 315 students ranked, students most commonly identified class discussion (26.0%), homework (16.2%), attendance (8.6%), and paying attention. Of the 282 students who identified a third most important activity, 17.8% listed class discussion, 16.7% listed homework, 8.5% listed attendance, and 7.1% listed paying attention. And finally, homework (15%), attendance (11.1%), class discussion (9.7%), and paying attention (9.2%) were most commonly listed as the fourth most important activity by the 207 students who provided a response. While these percentages may seem low, they also attest to the wide variety of activities that students listed.

When students were asked how they believe that their instructor grades participation, the majority of the 336 students who responded (44.9%) either referred me to previous questions they had answered or simply listed the same activities they had already identified. However, 18.8% of students admitted that they did not know how participation was graded, which may also have been true of those students who simply re-listed activities. Of the remaining students who answered this question, 4.2% said from memory, 6.8% said from observation, 2.7% said it wasn't graded, 6.8% said that points were given, and 15.8% simply offered descriptions such as fairly, generously, or by effort.

Instructor Results

When asked to list everything that counts toward the participation grade for their class, the majority of the instructors listed class discussion (75.0%) and in-class writing (55.0%) (See Table 3). Interestingly, two of the four instructors who said that participation did not make up a percentage of the course grade still chose to list activities when asked what counted toward the participation grade. When asked what they most valued, instructors often ranked attendance as being most important for participation, with 40% listing this activity first. Other activities listed first included in-class writing, class discussion, group work, and homework.

When instructors were asked how they graded participation, the most common response was said to be by observing students during class (20.0%). Other responses were by taking notes (15.0%), by adding points (15.0%), by rounding/not rounding up the grade (10.0%), by peer review (10.0%), and by not grading (10.0%). Each of the following responses was given by 5.0% of instructors: check marks, graded written responses, and by giving the student what he/she deserves. These responses, in addition to details about why instructors chose to grade participation, will be discussed in detail in the next section.

Activity	Number of instructors out of 20 who included this activity	Percentage of instructors who included this activity
Class Discussion	15	75.0%
In-class Writing	11	55.0%
Group Work	7	35.0%
Attendance	5	25.0%
Peer Critique	4	20.0%
Asking questions	3	15.0%
Stay alert	2	10%
Nothing	2	10%
Misc. (effort, presentations, laughing, reading, respect, debates, motivation)	1 each	5.0%

Table 3. *Activities Instructors Count Toward Participation Grade*

Discussion

It is somewhat surprising that the majority of students reproduced that they had no idea what their participation was worth in their composition courses. Even though this information could probably be found on the students' course syllabi, the students' lack of knowledge about this grade was disconcerting simply because participation was usually worth enough to alter the students' final grade, often somewhat substantially. However, because students were so varied in their responses to what they believed participation meant in this course, it appears that the majority of students seemed to have only a slight understanding of what was expected of them. And ironically, many students were also unaware that participation was *not* being graded in some of these classes, often listing various activities they believed counted toward this grade when in fact none did. However, students might have been inclined to believe that their participation would be graded due to past experiences in high school or other college courses.

Students and instructors seemed to be in some agreement about what participation meant, although major discrepancies were still apparent. Class discussion was a common expectation among both students and instructors, which was not surprising as participation is often used interchangeably with discussion in the previous studies I reviewed. Attendance and homework were also listed often, although there was disagreement among instructors about the relation of these activities to participation. One instructor wrote, "Some students assume that things like being present in class and having completed a reading response count as participation; they don't, and I make sure that students know that." Initially, it was surprising that so many instructors ranked attendance first, as this seems contradictory to what we know about active learning requiring more than one's presence in class. Of course, it is likely that instructors saw attendance as a necessary precursor to other activities, and this seemed to be reaffirmed in instructors' discussions of grading, as no instructor actually mentioned attendance as a necessary factor. Yet many students listed *only* attendance, suggesting that many students felt that simply being in class was enough. Unfortunately, this finding seems to be consistent with those of the previously mentioned study on student disengagement (see Bauerlein), as students may come to class but not see any reason to become involved with classroom activities.

Even more perplexing than beliefs about attendance was the finding that so many students and even a few instructors saw homework as being a relevant part of a participation grade. Homework, an out-of-class activity, does not seem to be a way for students to participate in class. But grading out-of-class activities does not seem to be uncommon, as professors often include these activities as a part of the participation grade (Bean and Peterson). Yet one instructor who did not grade participation wrote, "The students receive credit for turning in their rewrites as we do them. For more in-depth homework assignments, I may assign a 2 or a 1 as a grade for effort. But that isn't really participation, is it?" Apparently, many students and instructors thought that completing homework was a way for students to participate, possibly due to a belief that students were then better prepared to do in-class activities.

Perhaps the most intriguing results, however, were those produced by the questions about grading. Instructors valued rather vague activities for participation. How, one might ask, does an instructor grade a student for things such as effort, looking alert, or even contributing to class discussions? Or how might an instructor grade a student for in class writing, when the instructor rarely sees the end result? Students were by far the most perplexed by the question about grading, as shown by the fact that nearly half of the students simply repeated the same activities that they listed in response to previous questions. In fact, some students even seemed irritated by this question, often referring me back to previous questions. One student even went so far as to write, "This question is redundant," failing to see that identifying *what* activities were being graded for participation is not the same thing as understanding *how* those activities were being graded.

Even those students who attempted to answer this question gave unsatisfying responses. Many students admitted to having no idea how their participation was being graded, although some displayed a degree of humor in their comments. One student wrote, "Hopefully, generously. Other than that I'm not sure," while another stated, "Not sure, but I hope I get an A." Other students showed slight worries about their lack of knowledge, writing, "I don't even know. I have no idea if all the volunteering I have done in class is even counting towards participation," and, "I hope/think it's just attendance" (It was not). One student quite bluntly wrote: "I don't know how people grade anything, so I couldn't tell you." Some students also displayed a perhaps overly confident belief about how their participation was being graded, writing "As long as you don't fall asleep or have never talked, you will be alright," and "He's not too harsh on us; very lenient." While these answers more precisely attempted to answer the question of how rather than what, they still show that students were, overall, confused.

Many students believed that participation was graded based on the instructors' general observations of them during class. Several students made comments to this end, expressing views such as the following: "I think she just at the end of the grading period goes through each student's name and tries to recall events to give a grade. Possibly some bias involved"; "It is a random thought. No actual evidence just based on her recollection of your participation"; "I don't think there's a grading criteria on participation. I think the grade is probably her opinion"; "I think at the end of the quarter they think back on each person and how outspoken and involved they were during the quarter and judge the grade accordingly"; "[I'm] not really all that sure. I think it is more of a feel thing that she will come up with at the end of the quarter." Perhaps these comments are the most disturbing, as they suggest that students felt that they had little control over their grade.

Unfortunately, the students' beliefs that the grading would be based on the instructor's observation of them were perhaps the most accurate of any expressed in response to the survey. One student wrote in response to my question on grading, "Why don't you just ask them yourself?" Having done so (although not upon the recommendation of the student), I found that the instructors were often no more specific in their answers than the students and were at times even contradictory. Basing the participation grade upon the instructors' perception of the students was not uncommon; instructors provided responses such as the following: "It's quite subjective, frankly. I emerge from the quarter with a general impression of each student's participation"; "I give one participation and attendance grade at the end of the quarter based on 2 things – 1) attendance 2) a general impression of the student's participation level throughout the quarter"; "I'm afraid I can't be very specific. I assign a grade that I feel the student deserves"; "I grade based on my impressions, on how well I 'know' the students at the end of the quarter, how much they talk and how much effort they put forth"; "Overall impression from each student. I consider their contributions in both class discussion and group work." These responses, obviously highly subjective, lack a solid explanation of how this grade is determined. But Bean and Peterson note that in their "informal discussions with professors . . . most professors determine participation grades impressionistically, using class participation largely as a fudge factor in computing final course grades" (33), so perhaps this type of instructor response should not be too surprising.

Other responses from instructors were equally vague. One instructor claimed: "I will count the points for the most eligible candidate and deduct points from those who fail to meet the standard." This seems problematic for at least two reasons: only one student can receive the full points for participation, and students did not seem to know that their participation grades were curved. Another instructor wrote: "Participation is not an end of the quarter grade. Students may get as many as 4 check marks/week. At the end of the quarter check marks are counted." But how does a student get a check mark? And how many check marks are needed to receive the full participation points? An equally vague response involved rewarding students by altering their final grades, with instructors writing, "I either round up or don't round up the grade depending on participation," and "In practice, some students receive an additional 'bump' if I consider them to be engaged members in class, but I don't penalize introverted students." While at least this grading method does not punish students, the use of the participation grade as a reward is problematic. Students may see participation as an extra, rather than necessary, part of learning and thus refrain from becoming involved if they feel they can receive a good grade regardless of how much they participate.

But the most disconcerting response about grading practices came from an instructor who explained the participation grade in rather contradictory terms. In response to one question, the instructor initially wrote, "To count for full participation, if they are generally alert and awake I'll give them full points." But this same instructor, when asked about grading, stated, "If they have no marks against them and they talk in class they get the full 100 points. If they have no marks and don't talk, they get 90 points." It cannot be that the students can both get full points just for being alert and awake and also lose points for not talking, as talking is not necessarily a part of being alert and awake.

Since there was such a discrepancy among students and even instructors about these expectations and grading practices, one cannot help but to question why participation needs to be included as a part of the composition course grade. After all, several instructors chose not to include it, and they voiced no complaints about a lack of engagement. Perhaps the most unique method of encouraging participation came from one instructor who did not include participation in the course grade: "On the first day of class, I explained that I expected students to participate in group work and in class writing projects. If they declined to participate, I would ask them to leave and mark the day as an absence (This has never happened)." This approach might help to increase student accountability, as participation is no longer a specific grade to be earned but an expectation for those who come to class. Elbow believes "that when we 'motivate' students with grades, we are not building motivation but undermining it: we are gradually *sapping* the ability to work or think or wonder under their own steam" (13). It is true with the case of the aforementioned instructor that students' course grades can still be affected if students are being marked absent when they fail to participate, but it is also true that her expectations for participation are much clearer than any other instructor surveyed. This instructor justified her method as follows: "I don't count it as a grade because I see my role as instructional leader in the classroom. To that end, I use a variety of strategies to motivate students intrinsically to participate when possible, and to draw out reluctant students. I'm not comfortable grading students on participation, because I don't see a way to make those kinds of expectations reliably quantifiable." Based on the vague responses from other instructors, it seems that making this grade quantifiable is indeed challenging. And this is problematic, as this inability to clarify expectations for students may encourage them to feel less in control of their grades and therefore less inclined to think critically in the writing classroom. If instructors are unable to explain how they grade this fairly significant portion of the overall course grade, then perhaps instructors need to consider how this lack of clarity might disadvantage their students.

The instructors seemed to have good intentions for grading participation, and most instructors seemed to be in agreement about why they chose to include participation in their course grade. A common justification given by instructors was that participation was always included in the courses they took as students. Other instructors seemed to fear that without a participation grade, students would choose not to be involved with the class: "It's sort of put out there that students won't talk if they aren't directly graded on it. I think I'm too afraid to try it (going without the participation grade that is)." While it may be true that students will participate less if they are not graded for it, it may also be true that this fear is unfounded; as mentioned before, the majority of students saw participation as an expected part of the course even when it was not graded. One student even wrote, "He just wants all of his students to learn so as long as we're all participating we're all learning." And it seems that this is why the instructors chose to grade participation—to encourage students to engage in the classroom. The instructors' goals for including participation are clearly worthwhile, and several of the goals instructors provided in their responses are worth listing in their entirety:

> "I count it to encourage lively discussions and to foster a stronger sense of community. Participation increases learning and retention of new knowledge, so I consider it an important component of success in the classroom."

"It's a largely discussion-oriented class and would fail without participation. I've learned through experience—I've never had an English class as an undergrad or grad that didn't emphasize participation."

"I count participation as part of the course grade because the students have to discuss and if they didn't have to participate then they probably wouldn't discuss."

"As courses like 151 depend so much upon the involvement and contribution of the students, it is absolutely desirable that a participation grade be there. I have always felt that some students deserve to be considered more generously than others. However, I don't let allow anything of a personal or sentimental/subjective kind to interfere with my evaluation. The discretion is acquired purely during the term."

"I genuinely believe that regular participation results in a more fun and more successful classroom experience for my students as well as for me. To me participation is not some arbitrary category of 'college requirements.' I want to encourage and recognize those students who help make class fun and interesting while punishing (to some degree) those who are unwilling or unable to make a contribution. To me it's like hosting a party: some folks in attendance will help make the party successful and fun while others refuse to contribute to the environment and prefer to stay in the corner of the room as spectators. It seems there are always givers and takers, but I want there to be as many givers as possible."

What is perhaps most interesting about these comments is that the first three instructors explained why they feel that participation is necessary rather than why they grade it, while the remaining two instructors showed a belief that grading participation is necessary in order to manage the classroom. It may be possible that the former instructors chose to include graded participation in the composition classroom because it is a tradition rather than because of an actual need to do so. And the latter instructors seemed to fear a classroom without a nebulous participation grade with which to maintain control. One of Stupinsky et al.'s recommendations, based on the results of their own study, is for instructors to create a high-control environment for their students, and providing clear expectations for earning a participation grade is one crucial factor in creating such an environment. However, if instructors want their students to be inclined to think critically, and the above statements seem to indicate that they do, then instructors may need to return some control to the students by making their expectations for participation more explicit, if they choose to grade participation at all.

Despite the limited size of my study, it has uncovered many troubling beliefs about participation among composition instructors and students and about nebulous grading practices among instructors. Studies such as my own may be especially useful in composition courses that depend on participation and are not often lecture-based. In addition, further studies are necessary to determine how different methods of grading participation affect students in terms of motivation, effort, and a disposition to think critically. Specifically, research needs to be done which compares composition classes that use participation grades to those that do not. Such studies would help to clarify whether participation grades are in fact needed to maintain control over students, or whether it may be more beneficial to give additional control to the students, as it may actually help them to succeed academically.

Implications

Instructors in this study seemed to desire primarily two things: engagement among the students and a way to encourage this engagement. Grading participation seems to be a tool used by many instructors to achieve this result, but student engagement achieved this way may come at the expense of the students. If it is true, as Stupinsky et al. suggest, "that creating a high control environment during the first year of college fosters a critical thinking disposition and bolsters academic success" (527), then it seems that instructors have reason to make participation requirements more tangible for students. If instructors do this, students may come to feel more in control of their ability to meet this expectation and thus develop a greater tendency to use critical thinking skills. But of equal importance is the possibility that students may simply become more motivated, as Perry et al. found that "compared with their moderate-control counterparts, high-academic-control students exerted more effort, reported less boredom and anxiety, expressed greater motivation, used self-monitoring strategies more often, felt more control over their course assignments and life in general, believed they performed better at the beginning and end of their course, and obtained higher final grades" (785). These desirable student outcomes alone are possible reasons to consider increasing student control by providing more explicit requirements for participation.

Because many students in this study believed that coming to class and doing homework were enough to earn participation points, it may be that students saw themselves as passive learners. But most instructors wanted students involved *in class* as well, and this is not surprising, as I cannot imagine a composition instructor who would not desire some form of participation from his/her students. While some students may choose to engage in the course regardless of the grade, other students may choose not to engage if they do not believe that their efforts matter. And why would they consider their efforts to be worthwhile if their grade is simply the result of their instructors' opinion of them? Stupinsky et al. argue, "First-year college students experience a substantial transition from high school to college that involves increased responsibilities in a new and challenging environment. These early experiences can make some students feel 'out of control' leading them to perceive college as a low-control environment characterized by academic struggles" (514). Freshman composition is often one of the first college experiences that a student has, and if academic control helps students to become better students, then composition instructors have reason to help their students to gain this control.

Because there does not seem to be a way to make the participation grade quantifiable enough for students to feel control over this course requirement, there is reason to suppose that participation should not be a part of a student's freshman composition grade. It may be important to note here that it is the grading of participation, not the act, of which I am wary. Elbow, who sees all grading as problematic anyway, argues that grades are not trustworthy, often have unclear meaning, and are difficult to determine (6). And whether or not this is true of *all* grading, his belief seems to be confirmed with regard to participation by my findings, as his description adequately describes the grading processes of the instructors I surveyed. While grading is often a subjective, slightly frustrating process anyway, it becomes even more challenging when trying to grade student participation. Many of these instructors claimed to rely on a feeling, and it is, after all, unclear as to as to how a feeling translates into a grade. It is not surprising that Elbow believes that "conventional grading often makes students feel a bit mystified, helpless, and even paranoid about what they will 'get' for the course" (10). This description is not that of a student who feels in control of his/her grade, and perhaps this inability to make the participation grade quantifiable for the student is "why assessment and measurement scholars almost universally advise *against* grading class participation" (Bean and Peterson 33).

When I completed a pilot study for this project, my grading of participation was much like those of the instructors discussed above: a completely subjective tool used to alter students' grades to my liking. It was also a way to make me feel more in control of my course. Because I became unsure about my own practice of grading participation, in the following quarters I awarded each student all of the possible participation points out of guilt, as I felt that I could not adequately judge their participation when I was so unsure about it myself. Later, I tried asking students to turn in pieces of paper each day telling me what they did to participate. Yet this method still came down to my own opinion of the students, and I began to question why grading participation is even necessary. Deciding to practice what I preach, I chose not to grade participation in my current class, and I can honestly say that students are no less engaged than before. The only difference that I see is that I no longer have to worry about how to grade this troublesome component. Elbow challenges us with the following questions for consideration: "Instead of asking, 'Grading – yes or no?' let's ask, 'Grading – when and how much?'" ("Taking" 7). Perhaps participation should not be graded in the composition classroom, as it is apparently difficult to quantify and confusing to define. At the very least, instructors need to make their expectations and requirements for the participation grade as explicit as possible, even if this means relinquishing the control that comes from having a nebulous participation grade. As a result, students might feel greater control over their grade, thus resulting in increased motivation, engagement, and a disposition to think critically.

Notes

1. In most classes, participation is included as a part of a student's course grade, with a study at one university finding that 93 percent of all courses included this grade factor (Bean & Peterson).

2. According to Fritschner, "Breathing and staying awake were *level one. Level two* included students who came to class, took notes, and did the assignments. The *third level* included writing papers that were reflective and thoughtful. *Level four* included asking questions in class, making comments, and providing input for class discussions. The *fifth level* was doing additional kinds of research or coming to class with additional questions, and *level six* included oral presentations where the students themselves became the teachers" (354).

3. Stupnisky et al. focused their study on students' "disposition to think critically" (514), as this disposition is meant "to ensure the development and use of critical thinking skills" (515). They define perceived academic control as "a person's general belief in his or her capacity to influence and predict some aspect of the environment" (515).

Works Cited

Auster, Carol J., and Mindy MacRone. "The Classroom as a Negotiated Social Setting: An Empirical Study of the Effects of Faculty Members' Behavior on Students' Participation." *Teaching Sociology* 22.4 (1994): 289-300. Print.

Bauerlein, Mark. "A Very Long Disengagement." *The Chronicle of Higher Education.* 6 Jan. 2006. Web. 2 July 2008 .

Bean, John C. *Engaging Ideas: The Professor's Guide to Integrating Writing, Critical Thinking, and Active Learning in the Classroom.* San Francisco: Jossey-Bass Inc, 1996. Print.

———, and Dean Peterson. "Grading Classroom Participation." *New Directions for Teaching and Learning* 74 (1998): 33-40. Print.

Bruffee, Kenneth A. "Collaborative Learning and the 'Conversation of Mankind.'" *College English* 46.7 (Nov 1984): 635-52. Print.

Crombie, Gail, et al. "Students' Perceptions of Their Classroom Participation and

Instructor as a Function of Gender and Context." *The Journal of Higher Education* 74.1 (Jan 2003): 51-76. Print.

Elbow, Peter. "Taking Time Out from Grading and Evaluating While Working in a Conventional System." *Assessing Writing* 4.1 (1997): 5-27. Print.

———. *Writing Without Teachers*. London:Oxford UP, 1973. Print.

Fassinger, Polly A. "Understanding Classroom Interaction: Students' and Professors' Contributions to Students' Silence." *The Journal of Higher Education* 66.1 (1995): 82-96. Print.

Fritschner, Linda Marie. "Inside the Undergraduate College Classroom: Faculty and Students Differ on the meaning of Participation." *The Journal of Higher Education* 71.3 (2000): 342-62. Print.

Halpern, Diane F. "Teaching for Critical Thinking: Helping College Students Develop the Skills and Dispositions of a Critical Thinker." *New Directions for Teaching and Learning* 80 (1999): 69-74. Print.

McKeachie, Wilbert J. "Research on College Teaching: The Historical Background." *Journal of Educational Psychology* 82.2 (1990): 189-200. Print.

Murray, Donald M. "Write before Writing." *College Composition and Communication* 29.4 (1978): 375-81. Print.

Nunn, Claudia E. "Discussion in the College Classroom." *The Journal of Higher Education* 67.3 (1996): 243-66. Print.

Perry, Raymond P, et al. "Academic Control and Action Control in the Achievement of College Students: A Longitudinal Field Study." *Journal of Educational Psychology* 93.4 (2001): 776-89. Print.

Ryan, Gina J., Leisa L. Marshall, and Haomiao Jia. "Peer, Professor and Self-Evaluation of Class Participation." *Active Learning in Higher Education* 8.1 (2007): 49-61. Print.

Smith, Daryl G. "College Classroom Interactions and Critical Thinking." *Journal of Educational Psychology* 69.2 (1977): 180-90. Print.

Stupnisky, Robert H., et al. "The Interrelation of First-Year College Students' Critical Thinking Disposition, Perceived Academic Control, and Academic Achievement." *Research in Higher Education* 49.6 (2008): 513-30. Print.

Tobin, Lad. "Process Pedagogy." *A Guide to Composition Pedagogies*. Ed. Gary Tate, Amy Rupiper, and Kurt Schick. New York: Oxford UP, 2001. 1-18. Print.

Trimbur, John. "Consensus and Difference in Collaborative Learning." *College English* 51.6 (1989): 602-16. Print.

Tsui, Lisa. "Fostering Critical Thinking Through Effective Pedagogy: Evidence from Four Institutional Case Studies." *The Journal of Higher Education* 73.6 (2002): 740-63. Print.

Appendix A

Participation in English 151 – Instructor Survey
Course/Section number _____

1. How much is participation worth in this class? _____

2. Did you explain to students what you expect for participation in this class?

YES   NO

If you checked yes, when did you explain this to your students?

3. What do you count toward the participation grade in this class? Please explain in detail.

4. Please list, in order of importance, the top four things students need to do in order to receive credit for participation in this class.

    1._____
    2._____
    3._____
    4._____

5. How do you encourage participation in your class? Please be specific.

6. Is it possible for students to lose participation points? How?

7. How do you grade participation at the end of the quarter? Please be as specific as possible.

8. Why do you count participation as a part of the course grade? Were you taught that it should be a part of the course grade? If so, when?

Appendix B

Participation in English 151 – Student Survey
Course/Section Number _____

1. What percentage of your grade in this class is based on participation?

_____

2. Did your instructor explain what he/she expects in terms of participation for this class?

        YES   **NO**

If you checked yes, please explain what your instructor said as best as you can remember.

3. What do you think your instructors counts as participation in this class? Please list everything that you think counts toward your participation grade.

4. Please list, in order of importance, the top four things you believe you must do in order to receive participation points in this class.

        1._____
        2._____
        3._____
        4._____

5. How does your instructor encourage participation in this class?

6. How do you think that your instructor grades participation? Please be as specific as possible.

English 109.02:
Intensive Reading and Writing II, "Reading, Writing, Blogging"

Ben McCorkle

1. Course Description

English 109.02 is the second of a three-course basic writing track available to all students at The Ohio State University, Ohio's largest public university and flagship institution, which in total serves approximately 45,000 undergraduate students across all campuses. While the Columbus campus places students into the course based on a preliminary essay assessment, the Marion regional campus works according to a model of self-placement, where students decide whether or not to take the course based on an informed self-assessment of their individual skills and needs. The course description on the departmental website says that the course "provides intensive practice in integrating academic reading and writing." Within certain curricular guidelines, there is a good deal of freedom in terms of individual course design. The theme of my particular course is blogging and the citizen-journalist movement.

2. Institutional Context

As a land grant institution, The Ohio State University is open admissions, a status that is bestowed exclusively on the regional campuses while Columbus has tightened admissions standards over the past decade. Consequently, we at the Marion campus often get a caliber of student that is not quite fully prepared for the workload and rigor of college-level study. Our campus population consists of approximately 1,500 undergraduate students, which includes a mixture of traditional students with insufficient GPAs and ACT scores to warrant acceptance to the Columbus campus (but who will eventually move to the Columbus campus if their performance after several quarters merits it); older, nontraditional students who work, have children, and have not entertained academic pursuits for some time; and students for whom English is neither their native spoken nor written language. For this mixed demographic, retention is a central concern, and our campus is committed to creating conditions to ensure retention from the very beginning of a student's experience on the Marion campus. As we see it, this challenge involves balancing multiple factors—accommodating students' skills-based needs, instilling in them an interest in college-level work, and helping them feel like an empowered, integral part of the university community—and thus requires that we address it in a variety of ways at the administrative level as well as in our individual classrooms.

Students on the Marion campus self-place into first-year writing (110) or basic writing courses (109.01 and 109.02), a policy the English faculty maintains because we believe it empowers students to become active, accountable participants in their own educational process. The system also minimizes the negative stigma so often associated with remedial or basic writing courses. Typically, incoming students attend a placement orientation session, during which they learn about the distinctions among the three classes from which they can select, ask the coordinators questions to help fully inform their decision, and conduct a self-diagnostic based upon their own assessment of their skills as student writers. Once that decision has been made, students that chose to take 109.01 will have a midterm conference with their instructors, where they will discuss whether 109.02 or 110 will be a more appropriate option for them. While the goal of this system is to provide students with the conditions necessary to make an honest, informed decision about the writing courses they should take, the ultimate decision lies with the individual student, and sometimes that decision is made based upon factors such as schedule, money (credit hours don't "count" towards graduation for 109 courses), or peer pressure—in other words, what we might deem contaminating factors. Because of the tendency for underprepared writers to opt out of taking basic writing courses, the basic writing instructors collectively recognize that they have to do a good job of selling their courses to the students. For example, for my 109.02 course, I crafted a short video commercial (located at http://www.youtube.com/watch?v=AhCmSDexH-s) that I distributed to 109.01 instructors to pass along to their students.

The rhetoric and composition faculty at Marion has been working to expand the conception of writing on the campus, both among the general faculty and the student body at large, to include more than just literary analysis, personal narratives, and traditional forms of creative writing such as poetry and short fiction. In one respect, we have become advocates of multimodal composing, purposeful and rhetorically aware combinations of alphabetic text with sound, still images, and video. This focus is present in many of our course offerings, from basic writing to upper-level classes. Additionally, we have been working to address the need for increased opportunities for our students to engage in more civic or public writing, seen most recently in our establishment of a writing minor (available for any major) accompanied by various internships with area nonprofit organizations, local newspapers, and the like. In addition to offering students professionalizing opportunities for the future (Marion is located in an economically distressed portion of the state, a mix of rust-belt and rural areas), we feel such adjustments help our program as well. My particular basic writing course contains both the public writing and new media themes. By incorporating these themes in a lower-level writing course, my goal is to create continuity between basic writing and upper-level writing courses rather than have the course appear cordoned off from (and perhaps deemed inferior to) the "real" writing courses. As many of our basic writing students end up becoming English majors or declaring writing minors later on, this type of integration helps to create potential new recruits for our program by introducing them to our writing program's broader culture and curricular objectives right from the start.

3. Theoretical Rationale

One of my main goals when designing my version of 109.02 was to create a course that had a relevant, timely topic and would allow students the chance to explore that topic in both analytic and productive capacities (i.e., as both readers and writers). The blog, approached in this course as an object of inquiry as well as a writing space, seemed like the ideal theme because of the genre's inherent plasticity. As Michael Banks writes in his 2008 book *Blogging Heroes*, the blog has emerged as and matured into a viable online communications genre "[b]ecause blogging is dynamic and flexible, and at its core, blogging is a communications tool that encompasses all communication models: one-to-one, one-to-many, many-to-one, and many-to-many" (xx). Moreover, a central rhetorical lesson I try to impart to basic writing students is an awareness of audience and how to write for a variety of them by developing a distinctive voice in their writing, a feature endemic to blogging; again, as Banks emphasizes, "Spreading their presence around the world is exactly what bloggers are doing. Whether the blogger is an individual or a corporation, government, or other institution, the idea is the same: establish and spread a presence" (xx).

"Reading, Writing, Blogging" therefore focuses on the citizen-journalist movement as it is realized in the blogosphere and approaches the topic using multiple lines of inquiry: What social/cultural factors have led to the emergence of this new genre of writing? How does the genre function formally? What common rhetorical traits appear in the writing across multiple examples? How does this new genre differ from earlier types of journalism, personal writing, memoir, log-keeping, etc.? What role does the changing face of technology play in shaping the citizen-journalist movement? To those ends, I included a variety of texts to foster thought and discussion on the topic, including selections from the online collection *Into the Blogosphere*, excerpts from Suzanne Stefanac's *Dispatches from Blogistan*, Chuck Olsen's documentary film *Blogumentary*, and Dan Gillmor's *We the Media: Grassroots Journalism By the People, For the People* (an excellent, thorough take on the subject, and written clearly enough for an audience not accustomed to regular reading). I assigned the class two major formal writing assignments (each of them three to four pages in length) for the term. The first, a rhetorical analysis of a blog of their own choosing, asked them not only to describe the content of the selected blog, but also to identify its overall purpose (to inform, persuade, amuse, or perhaps a combination of purposes), characterize the blog's audience (based not only on suppositions gleaned from the topic and writing style, but also on actual reader comments, outbound links, and other ancillary data), and describe the formal elements of the blog (font style, color scheme, graphics, and so on), addressing how well such elements coordinated with the blog's content. The second assignment, a chance to expose students to an additional generic staple of academic discourse, asked them to write a critical review of Gillmor's *We The Media*; more than a "thumbs up/thumbs down" opinion piece, the goal of this assignment was to compose a studied evaluation of the book that considered its strong points as well as weak points; assessed its main argument; and provided support for those claims by either specifically referencing details from the book itself or citing additional reviews, blog posts, or other external reactions to it.

Additionally, I assigned several informal writing tasks that students posted to our online discussion board on the university's course-management system; these writing tasks offered students the opportunity to develop ideas, generate summaries of readings, ponder questions about the connections between rhetorical analysis and the rhetorical considerations they were making while building and writing for their own blogs, and broadly raise thematic questions on course content in a low-stakes writing venue. Time spent in class was divided between discussing assigned readings, often tying them to recent events or stories in the news, and studio sessions, where students would work on their own blogs. These blogs were set up using the free web service Vox (http://www.vox.com) because it is user-friendly and allows users to define different degrees of access to the blog (fully public, fully private, or open to a select "neighborhood" of readers). Students could either singly or collaboratively write the blogs, and they needed to be on a newsworthy topic that interests the student, preferably one that would sustain his or her interest for the duration of the course. Regular posting, the use of generic conventions such as hyperlinking or incorporating graphics/multimedia content, as well as commenting on their classmates' blogs were all expectations of this course component.

In a recent article for *Computers & Composition Online* co-written with Catherine Braun and Amie Wolf, I made the call for bringing digital media into the basic writing curriculum and articulated my rationale for why I thought this would be an effective pedagogical move. In it, I identified two main tenets for doing so:

1. This approach advocates for the production of digital media texts for its own sake. By now it is a well-rehearsed argument that the material boundaries of those texts that we call "writing" are expanding, slipping, and metamorphosing into entirely different shapes. Students need to become familiar with those shapes as they may be expected to produce these new types of texts in real-world contexts.

2. Digital media production also helps enhance students' conceptual understanding of the rhetorical process by rendering the familiar strange. The rhetorical dimensions of writing can often hide from students' views precisely because they have been for so long immersed in the written word. Armed with a new perspective of how a text's form or medium carries with it unique rhetorical considerations, students can employ this newly enhanced awareness within the conventional writing process. (Braun, McCorkle, and Wolf)

While I originally made those remarks within the context of the first basic writing course in the three-course sequence, the concept also informs how I think of 109.02, with some distinctions. In terms of quantity, students are expected to produce more alphabetic text than in 109.01; a course situated around blogging helps in this regard. In other words, even though blogging certainly invites the opportunity to engage with multimodal forms of communication, the genre as it exists today leans heavily towards the alphabetic text end of the continuum. Moreover, the blogging format, a curious hybrid of private, informal writing and public, formal writing, seemed to me to be especially accommodating to a variety of styles and skill levels, which makes it well suited as a writing environment in which basic writing students can grow comfortable, take chances, and develop as writers. Also, 109.02 aims to move students closer to producing academic discourse in particular, a focus of our first-year writing curriculum; my reading requirements, discussions, and assignment designs therefore reflect that emphasis. These components are not only quantitatively greater than the typical work a student might do in 109.01—longer reading assignments, longer page requirements for essays—they also challenge students to begin exercising the skills endemic to academic discourse, such as dense description and rhetorical analysis (as in the case of their first main essay) or summary and critical assessment (as in the case of their second main essay).

Two complementary ideas shape my pedagogical philosophy for every course I teach, and 109.02 is no exception. In one respect, I believe that learning best happens when we allow an element of play to infuse our classroom dynamic and assignments. Much like Albert Rouzie, I too feel that:

Despite the emergence of computer technology and its potential for enhancing the play element in literacy education, a normative ideology of work, reality, seriousness, practicality, and adult behavior continues to rule postsecondary institutions, blinding most educators to the significance of the play that is already occurring in their classrooms, preventing them from addressing it as a productive force for change and learning and from perceiving it as an interesting phenomenon in its own right. (Rouzie 629)

Additionally, the work we ask of our students should to some extent overlap with their "real life" concerns and present them with the opportunity to think of how their ideas fit into the public discourse. As Rosa Eberly advocates in her article "The Anti-Logos Doughball: Teaching Deliberating Bodies the Practices of Participatory Democracy," we must turn to more praxis-based ways of framing rhetorical instruction for our undergraduates in order to help them enter the world as engaged citizens. The classroom therefore becomes a safe space in which to practice the very kinds of discourse we hope our students will go on to produce later in their lives, and a climate of play encourages experimentation and chance-taking within that space. From the outset, I thought that a course thematically centered around blogging fit well with my pedagogy, for reasons I unpack in the following section.

It is my hope that this combination of principles would work well to target an at-risk population on our campus not only by enticing them to participate in the academic conversation because it could actually be fun (imagine!), but also by validating their voices as engaged citizens with real opinions on issues that matter to them. Consequently, when the course played out in real time, I made a concerted effort, and I believe to good effect, to regularly reinforce these ideas for the benefit of my students.

4. Critical Reflection

After a couple of weeks into the term, I discovered a bit more about the makeup of the students in my course. As is often the case with basic writing students, many of them expressed a dislike of writing, or at least indicated that it was an activity they didn't regularly do. The reasons for this were several: because it was too hard or they felt they weren't any good at it, because it was boring, or because past experiences with writing (and grading) had soured them on the entire enterprise. Additionally, many students admitted that they didn't follow the news (print, television, or otherwise) because they felt as if the topics covered didn't speak to their interests or their immediate social context enough. Finally, my students indicated that they had either marginal interest in technology, or a sporadic interest at best: while some students self-identified as outright technophobes who rarely interacted with the computer, others described a vigorous but compartmentalized interaction with computers that consisted predominantly of interacting on social networking sites like Facebook or MySpace, using instant messaging/chat applications, and watching videos on YouTube.

Given my students' uneasiness with matters of writing, the news media, and technology in general (an uneasiness that I had anticipated to some extent), I accordingly crafted my curriculum to address those concerns. For one, I wanted to help them grow more comfortable as writers, and blogging offered that opportunity, as it allows students a less formal writing space than the academic paper in which to experiment with voice, citing outside sources, and crafting arguments. The world of blogs can easily accommodate tones ranging from the most conservative and staid to the avant garde to the downright snarky. Secondly, I wanted to give students the opportunity to make their own news, to empower them as citizens with something to say about a particular topic that matters to them and their community—topics that might get overlooked by more official journalism outlets. Finally, my goal was to expose them to technology *as producers*, more so than their current habits of use indicate. To give students access to technology is a good first step, but it must be followed with exposing them to the range of possibilities of digital literacy; otherwise, they may not recognize their own potential for becoming active participants within this still-evolving technological landscape.

As the course played out over the following weeks, I would generally characterize the outcome as a classic case of mixed results and, on the whole, a satisfying experience. Some students were genuinely enthusiastic about their blog projects. For example, the trio of students who were into comic books and graphic novels went above and beyond expectations by making special trips to local comics stores to talk to managers, other comics fans, and even a couple of local artist/writers. One student, because a young niece had gotten lead poisoning from playing with a lead-painted toy, vigorously read into news stories about calls to strengthen toy safety standards, import controls, and the like. One of the strongest blogs was themed around recasting national news stories about how families deal with having active-duty relatives in the military through her own experiences dealing with her son, who was stationed in Iraq at the time. And while some topics were decidedly uninspired (i.e., topics such as "country music artists that I like" or "general musings about sports"), and while a couple of students benefited from gentle prodding on my part to stick to task, and one student in particular needed a lot of attention because he had an especially hard time generating topics to write about, most of the students kept up the pace of regular posting, commenting, and researching for the term's duration.

Keeping the motivation level high was an issue I worked on throughout the term, one that I addressed in a variety of ways. One technique involved embracing the concept of play. For example, I periodically asked student to craft their blog posts in keeping with popular (and fun) generic conventions:

drafting "ten best/worst" lists or picking a fight (respectably, of course) with a fellow blogger by writing a critical reply to a previous post, for instance. Additionally, I made sure to highlight the work of my students throughout the course, using particularly insightful blog posts, reading summaries, or essay paragraphs as models of good writing for the entire class to contemplate. I also exposed students to different forms and genres of texts in order to promote variety and sustain interest. In addition to Gillmor's text, I showed them a documentary film (Olsen's *Blogumentary*), paired conventional news coverage with blogosphere reactions on several recent topics (articles on the presidential primaries or local stories dealing with campus crime, for example), and even hosted an iChat webcam interview with a Missouri-based blogger who writes several blogs dealing with topics that range from educational technology to microbrewed beer reviews to the indie rock scene in Columbia, Missouri. For the most part, the students seemed to respond positively to these measures, a feeling which was confirmed by my end-of-term student evaluations. Students were particularly interested in getting to chat with a "real life" blogger, an experience which reinforced the public nature of their own writing. Despite its reliance on the "talking head" format, Olsen's film was slickly produced, offered a variety of opinions from prominent bloggers, and was generally well paced. Students also seemed to appreciate having their own writing held up as models of good practice; in addition to allowing students to develop ways of differentiating between more and less effective rhetorical and stylistic strategies in their writing, the move also allowed me to help validate their work as bona fide writers—the empowering effects of which aid in dispelling their own feelings of inadequacy brought on by the well documented stigmas associated with basic writing.

Because of the high degree of variability among blogs in the "real life" blogosphere (in terms of style, level of formality, length of posts, frequency of linking, or inclusion of multimodal elements), grading my students' blogs posed a challenge, one that I attempted to address by what I call a dense feedback loop between my students and me. In addition to paying attention to whether or not students met the quantifiable requirements—minimum number of posts, adequate length, adhering to specific requests to include graphics, link to an external source, and leaving comments on their classmates' blogs, I also conversed with them face to face and in writing via email or their blogs' comment sections. It was during such consultations that I pressed students to explain to me the rhetorical meta-concepts behind their blog's perceived purpose, imagined audience, strategies they employed to reach that audience, blogs in the wild they considered modeling their own after, and so on. I also asked them to demonstrate to me what they deemed material areas of growth or improvement as their blogs progressed, such as longer posts, more use of external sources, or a stronger sense of voice with more complex sentences, diction, and the like. Among the highlights of these conversations: one student explained to me how she began crafting a "snarkier" persona on her blog after classmates remarked that they enjoyed that aspect of her personality in class and missed it in her otherwise straightforward blogging style; one student, whose blog dealt with having an active-duty relative in the military, said she felt more comfortable relating news stories to her own experience as the term progressed, and began to blog more from that context; perhaps the weakest writer in the course, one student began the term writing less than 100 words per post, but increased to regularly over 250 words because, he claimed, of the encouraging comments on his blog. My goal here was two-fold: not only did I rely on these self-assessments to help me arrive at a grade for the blog, I also saw them as a tool for reinforcing rhetorical self-awareness of their own writing processes, with respect to their own blogs, certainly, but all the other types of writing they did in the course as well.

One area that's particularly tricky to navigate with basic writing students is the question of homework (as in, "How can I get them to do their homework?"). Generally, basic writing students have a notoriously hard time completing homework assignments, symptomatic of a lack of preparedness for the amped-up rigors of college-level education (as a colleague of mine is fond of saying, writing instruction is only *half* of the curriculum in the basic writing classroom, we also teach them how to be college students). Consequently, I work to meet them half-way. Aside from the major essays for the term, I gave my students fairly light, manageable homework assignments: find a newsworthy story covered by both an "official" journalism source and a blog to discuss in class, or create a blogroll of sites with a similar focus to the student's own blog.

Central to these case studies were in-class discussions focused upon how a writer's style or voice would differ depending on the intended audience or purpose for the piece in question; how, for example, an AP wire report might sound more generic and "facts first" in its tone because of its potential national readership in papers across the country, while a small-scale blogger's take on the same topic might be more personalized and opinionated because of a more intimate readership or a more explicit editorial purpose. Also, I structured class in such a way that the bulk of work could be started in the classroom. The last half of each class was designated "studio time," and during this hour, students could brainstorm ideas for topics to write about, work on blog posts and formal writing, and consult with me and fellow students about their writing (sustained conversation about writing, to my mind, is an effective way of fostering that crucial sense of rhetorical awareness in our students). While a few students certainly had problems with motivation even with these accommodations (as well as a couple of pointed after-class consultations), the vast majority of students responded well to this structure.

In-class discussion comprised a central component of the course, as is the case for most of my courses. Sure, students were engaged and on-point with many of the readings and topics that I anticipated—the Olsen film, excerpts from Stefanac's book, and the occasional snarky blog example such as Wonkette or Gawker—but there were some happily unanticipated hotspots as well, the biggest one being Miller and Shepherd's article "Blogging as Social Action: A Genre Analysis of the Weblog" from *Into the Blogosphere*, a piece I was sure would alienate them because of its relative density and the fact that it was written primarily for an audience of academics. Instead, the majority of the class really seemed captivated by the idea that genres emerge because of various cultural, political, and technological factors, and that we can talk about the development of the blog in terms of those social elements in addition to the formal qualities that characterize it (i.e., reverse chronology, text-heavy, two- or three-column layout, etc.). To say the least, I was proud that they had eagerly tackled such a sophisticated academic article so early in the term. In some instances, the discussions lagged, and this was often surrounding the reading selections from Gillmor's book, another unexpected result because I thought the book was so readable. In fact, I discovered early on that the students weren't relating to the specific examples Gillmor draws upon because they were either outdated or too specialized, such as the business blogger backlash against Qwest CEO Joe Nacchio, the grassroots uprising under Howard Dean's 2004 presidential bid, or the Jayson Blair *New York Times* story fabrication fiasco. Consequently, I made the adjustment to supplement Gillmor's examples with more up-to-date ones rather easily: given that the 2008 presidential primary season was in full swing at the time I taught the class and that there was a wide range of vigorously held opinions about the candidates among my students, this was a fairly easy course correction to implement.

I made conscious efforts to connect my students' blogging to their formal writing assignments in order to reinforce the array of rhetorical considerations that, indeed, connect all types of communication. Partly, this was structural—studio sessions in class included not only work on blogging assignments, but also work on their essays. This included collective brainstorming sessions on topics, where students would display their chosen blogs to analyze on the computer lab projector, offer some preliminary remarks indicating how they were thinking of approaching the analysis, and discussing this with the rest of the class. Further along, I had students show drafts-in-progress on the projector, where I would prompt the class to react to the global (structure, organization, etc.), as well as the local (style, sentence variety, etc.), aspects of the essays. On several occasions, the class was especially good about suggesting stylistic revisions to the drafts, indicating to me that they understood the differences in voice expected of academic writing and the oftentimes less formal style of blogging. I recall one student, in response to another's analysis of what he deemed a poorly done sports blog, offering up a much better example of the genre that the student ended up using as a counter-example in his essay. I also drew upon early discussions about the rhetorical impact of a blog's design—how audiences typically expect some degree of harmony between what a blog is *about* and its visual elements—to establish the context for talking about formal expectations of document design in traditional academic writing; I argued that just as certain negative examples of poorly designed blogs impacted our sense of the blogger's credibility (one anonymous girl's "indie rock" blog, for instance, featured the mainstream group Nickelback in its background graphic), sloppily formatted papers that didn't adhere to MLA specifications likewise affected how the content was likely to be received. The main conceptual point I attempted to drive home throughout our studio sessions is that the way one writes, the audience one is trying to address, and the physical shape of that writing all need to be considered anew with each new act of writing.

Finally, one aspect of the course I found to be immensely helpful was having an embedded teaching assistant/tutor (and for your tireless service in this capacity, I would be remiss if I did not publicly thank you by name, Tabitha Clark). This embedded T.A. component was essentially a pilot program for our basic writing sequence, where advanced undergraduates concurrently take a course on writing center tutoring method and theory. Because of the course's studio structure, the T.A. would regularly work with students either individually or in small groups, helping them with developing topics, working on style or surface-level issues, addressing technical problems, and generally raising rhetorical awareness for the class (to this last point, "choice" became our mantra for the term, the heuristic lens through which students' decisions were regularly examined when we asked them to reflect on their progress). Some of the more reticent students around me, I noticed, tended to respond to the T.A. more readily. This was not an entirely unexpected reaction, as some students are more comfortable opening up to tutors precisely because they straddle the line of demarcation separating teacher and student (they impart their expertise without the added pressure associated with evaluation or related exercises of power). In a post-mortem conversation with the T.A., I was struck by an observation she made connecting her own presence in the classroom with the course's central topic. She, like the citizen journalist who brings a new perspective, ethics, and politics to the practice of traditional journalism, was likewise a liminal figure, capable of operating within both spheres of the power dynamic, unsettling the status quo and empowering the students in the process. I recall being impressed by the parallel, especially since I hadn't explicitly picked up on it myself.

On balance, I would say that "Reading, Writing, Blogging" was a successful course (perhaps an obvious conclusion, otherwise I would not have necessarily felt compelled to write about it). I found the blogging format to be malleable enough to accommodate a variety of different topics, writing styles, and degrees of skill. While it scratched my itch for wanting a central multimodal component in the course, it was still sufficiently writerly so that I didn't feel like I was depriving my students of the skill development needed for future courses, both in English and beyond. Among the things I need to figure out as I refine the course design is making note of the idiosyncrasies of the VOX platform up front (although it is user-friendly as I noted earlier, there are some issues with how they name/categorize things and group blogs together within the platform that caused some initial confusion). I would also like to assign a bit more multimodal work than I did; whereas I only had them do two posts that incorporated a self-produced video, digital image, or sound file of their choosing, I would probably make that assignment more directed to ensure that students play around with the available technology a bit more than this class did. I'd also like to incorporate newer trends into the blog project as well, such as micro-blogging or photostream accompaniments (for instance, Twitter or Flickr). Still, I love the idea of teaching this course again soon. So much of its design is in concert with our mission: not only helping our campus's basic writers succeed within the classroom, but also to thrive as writers and thinkers once they move beyond it.

Works Cited

Banks, Michael A. *Blogging Heroes: Interviews with Thirty of the World's Top Bloggers*. Indianapolis: Wiley Publishing, 2008. Print.

Braun, Catherine, Ben McCorkle, and Amie Wolf. "Remixing Basic Writing: Digital Media Production & the Basic Writing Curriculum." *Computers and Composition Online* (2007): n. pag. Web. 15 Feb. 2008.

Eberly, Rosa A. "The Anti-Logos Doughball: Teaching Deliberating Bodies the Practices of Participatory Democracy." *Rhetoric and Public Affairs* 5 (2002): 287-300. Print.

Olsen, Chuck. *Blogumentary*. Online documentary film. Google Video. 29 Jan. 2007. Web. 15 Feb. 2008.

Rouzie, Albert. "The Dialectic of Work and Play: A Serio-Ludic Rhetoric for Composition Studies." *JAC*. 20.3 (2000): 627-58. Print.

SYLLABUS

English 109.02C | Intensive Reading & Writing II | Winter 2008 Syllabus

PROVOCATIONS:

> ON THE SOCIAL IMPORTANCE OF BLOGS: "WHAT HAPPENS WHEN YOU START SEEING THE WEB AS A MATRIX OF MINDS, NOT DOCUMENTS? NETWORKS BASED ON TRUST BECOME AN ESSENTIAL TOOL. YOU START EVALUATING THE RELEVANCE OF DATA BASED NOT ON SEARCH QUERY RESULTS BUT ON PERSONAL TESTIMONY."
> **—Steven Johnson, "Mind Share." *WIRED* (May 2003)**

> "FREEDOM OF THE PRESS IS LIMITED TO THOSE WHO OWN ONE."
> **—A.J. Liebling (in *We The Media*)**

> "IF YOU DON'T LIKE THE NEWS . . . GO OUT AND MAKE SOME OF YOUR OWN."
> **—Wes Nisker (IN *WE THE MEDIA*)**

Course Description:

English 109.02, like 109.01, is designed to prepare students for success in English 110: First-Year Composition. In this course, students will practice reading verbal texts, images, and other media forms analytically. Through a variety of formal and informal writing assignments, we will approach issues of grammar and correctness from a *rhetorical* perspective—that is, instead of focusing on "right" and "wrong" notions of grammar, we will develop an understanding of these conventions within the context of academic discourse. Additionally, students will gain some experience producing new media texts that combine visual, verbal, and aural elements.

English 109.01 requires a substantial amount of reading, writing, and analysis. Readings from our main text (*We The Media*) and other sources will establish a context for our discussions and a variety of formal and informal written assignments: What is the social significance of the blog (or "weblog," that ever-evolving genre of web-based writing that is part diary, part scrapbook, part newspaper, etc.)? How are news-related blogs helping to reshape the role of journalists and news media in our society? How do blogs unsettle the traditional roles of writer and reader? What signs can we see in the blogosphere that hint at or indicate new uses and forms of this technology in the future?

Course Objectives:

Students enrolled in English 109 at Marion should meet the following objectives:

- Engage in reading, analyzing, and composing a wide range of texts, including both formal academic texts and also informal "nonacademic" texts (audio files, web sites, comics, children's/young adult literature, oral histories, etc.)

- Engage in the full writing process, including textual invention, drafting, revising, and editing

- Discuss and share writing and reading with others and develop a rhetorical vocabulary for talking about writing

- Produce coherent, unified, and fully supported written texts that demonstrate primary research and original analysis

- Gain knowledge of academic conventions of usage and grammar

- Interact with digital media, including work with word processing; Internet-based research and communication; and the production of texts such as web pages, images, and sound files

Texts:
[Additionally, there will be a few short readings from various print and online sources, as well as a viewing of the documentary film *Blogumentary*.]

> DAN GILLMOR. *WE THE MEDIA: GRASSROOTS JOURNALISM BY THE PEOPLE, FOR THE PEOPLE*. SEBASTOPOL, CA: O'REILLY, 2004. **ISBN: 0-59600-7337**
> Lynne Troyka, ed. *Simon and Schuster Quick Access Reference for Writers*. 5th ed. 2005. **ISBN: 0-13195-2269**

Class Requirements:
Formal Writing Assignments. The main component of our coursework is made up of two formal writing assignments, essays designed to strengthen your writing and analytical thinking. One essay will be a book review of our main text for the course, while the other will be a rhetorical analysis of a blog that you select. We will discuss these assignments in further detail later in the quarter.

BLOG. YOU WILL KEEP YOUR OWN BLOG BASED ON A FOCUSED NEWS TOPIC THAT YOU WILL SELECT. YOU WILL POST TWO ENTRIES PER WEEK, AT LEAST 250 WORDS IN LENGTH, AND WE WILL DEVOTE SOME CLASS TIME TO THIS ACTIVITY. YOUR ENTRIES WILL

NOT SIMPLY BE STATIC WRITTEN RESPONSES—YOU WILL ACTUALLY USE THE GENERIC
CONVENTIONS OF BLOG WRITING IN YOUR OWN BLOG, WHICH MEANS THAT YOU WILL
SOMETIMES HYPERLINK TO OUTSIDE SOURCES, INCLUDE GRAPHICS OR OTHER MULTIMEDIA
CONTENT, AND EVEN COMMENT ON YOUR COLLEAGUES' WRITINGS.

Readings. Several readings are assigned throughout the quarter. We'll be
discussing and writing about these at length, so actually reading them is
essential to the functionality of our class. If it seems that we are having trouble
completing the readings for class, I will begin assigning impromptu quizzes that
will figure into the final participation grade.

Online Discussion Forum. Using OSU's Carmen course management system
software (located at: HTTP://CARMEN.OSU.EDU/) I'VE SET UP AN ONLINE DISCUSSION
FORUM TO BE USED OUTSIDE OF CLASS PROPER. DURING THE COURSE OF THE QUARTER,
YOU WILL POST AT LEAST ONCE PER WEEK ON THE ASSIGNED READINGS OR VIEWINGS.
THESE POSTS SHOULD ACCOMPLISH TWO GOALS: 1) THEY SHOULD PROVIDE A SYNOPSIS
OR SUMMARY OF THE READING SELECTION; 2) THEY SHOULD ALSO OFFER SOME SORT OF
COMMENTARY ON THE READING SELECTION (EX: DO YOU AGREE OR DISAGREE WITH THE
AUTHOR'S MAIN ARGUMENT? CAN YOU POINT OUT EXAMPLES THAT SUPPORT OR REFUTE
THE READING? CAN YOU DRAW CONNECTIONS TO PREVIOUS READINGS?). EACH POST
SHOULD BE THE EQUIVALENT OF 1–2 DOUBLE-SPACED PAGES (250–500 WORDS).

EVALUATION:

Personal Blog: 20%
Book Review: 30%
Blog Analysis: 30%
Online Disc./Part.: 20%
Total: 100%

[Institutional/Class Policies Omitted]

Daily Schedule:
It is your responsibility to keep current with this schedule, but
remember also that the schedule may change. Readings listed for
any particular day are to be completed in advance of that day; you
need to be prepared to discuss them in class.

Abbreviation Key:
   WTM = *We The Media*
   QA = *Quick Access Reference for Writers*

MONTH ONE:

Week 1	**[Class 1]** Class introductions & review of syllabus; Diagnostic essay **[Class 2] So what is a blog, anyway?** (Read Miller and Shepherd, "Blogging as Social Action" from *Into the Blogosphere*) http://blog.lib.umn.edu/blogosphere/blogging_as_social_action_a_genre_analysis_of_the_weblog.html INTRODUCTION TO CARMEN (OSU's CONTENT MANAGEMENT SYSTEM SOFTWARE)
WEEK 2	**[CLASS 3] STARTING OUR OWN BLOGS:** TOPIC-DEVELOPMENT AND TECHNICAL WORKSHOP ON VOX BLOGGING PLATFORM **[CLASS 4] WTM:** (INTRODUCTION); **BLOG ANALYSIS** PROMPT ASSIGNED
WEEK 3	**[CLASS 5] WTM:** (CHAPTER 1); DISCUSSION AND WORKSHOPPING OF BLOG ANALYSIS ESSAY; BLOGGING STUDIO **[CLASS 6] WTM:** (CHAPTER 2); BLOGGING STUDIO; ALSO READ GALLO, "WEBLOG JOURNALISM" FROM *INTO THE BLOGOSPHERE* HTTP://BLOG.LIB.UMN.EDU/BLOGOSPHERE/WEBLOG_JOURNALISM.HTML
Week4	**[Class 7] WTM:** (Chapters 3 & 4); blogging studio **[CLASS 8] BLOG ANALYSIS ESSAY DUE;** BLOGGING STUDIO

MONTH TWO:

Week 5	**[Class 9] WTM:** (Chapters 5 & 6); blogging studio **[CLASS 10]** MIDTERM EVALUATIONS; READ STEFANAC, *DISPATCHES FROM BLOGISTAN* (EXCERPT TBD)
WEEK 6	**[CLASS 11] WTM:** (CHAPTERS 7 & 8); BLOGGING STUDIO **[CLASS 12] BOOK REVIEW** PROMPT ASSIGNED; BRAINSTORMING/DRAFTING SESSION FOR BOOK REVIEWS
WEEK 7	**[CLASS 13] WTM:** (CHAPTERS 9 & 10); BLOGGING STUDIO **[Class 14] Anatomy of a Book Review** (Read McCorkle, "So Be the News, Already!") http://www.cwrl.utexas.edu/currents/fall05/mccorkle.html
WEEK 8	**[CLASS 15] WTM:** (CHAPTERS 11 & 12); TELECONFERENCE WITH **NAME REDACTED**, SEMI-PROFESSIONAL ÜBER-BLOGGER; BLOGGING TO BE DONE OUTSIDE OF CLASS **[CLASS 16] BOOK REVIEW** DUE; VIEWING: *BLOGUMENTARY.* COMMENT ON DOCUMENTARY IN CARMEN DISCUSSION FORUM (POSSIBLE PROMPTS INCLUDED IN THREAD)

MONTH THREE:

WEEK 9	[CLASS 17] FOLLOW-UP DISCUSSION ON *BLOGUMENTARY.* IN-CLASS STUDIO TIME [CLASS 18] IN-CLASS STUDIO TIME; INDIVIDUAL CONFERENCES ON REVISIONS TO PORTFOLIO; COURSE EVALUATIONS
WEEK 10	[CLASS 19] IN-CLASS STUDIO TIME; INDIVIDUAL CONFERENCES ON REVISIONS TO PORTFOLIO; COURSE EVALUATIONS [CLASS 20] IN-CLASS STUDIO TIME; WRAP-UP DISCUSSION; INDIVIDUAL CONFERENCES ON REVISIONS TO PORTFOLIO

FINALS WEEK	**FINAL PORTFOLIOS DUE NO LATER THAN 5 P.M.**

▥ The MIT Press

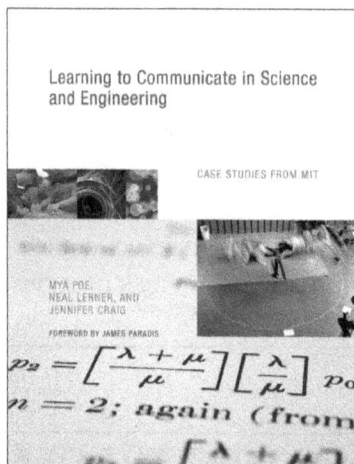

Learning to Communicate in Science and Engineering

CASE STUDIES FROM MIT

MYA POE,
NEAL LERNER, AND
JENNIFER CRAIG

FOREWORD BY JAMES PARADIS

$p_2 = \left[\frac{\lambda + \mu}{\mu}\right]\left[\frac{\lambda}{\mu}\right] p_0$

$n = 2;$ again (from

$\left[\frac{\lambda + \mu}{}\right]$

Learning to Communicate in Science and Engineering

CASE STUDIES FROM MIT

Mya Poe, Neal Lerner, and Jennifer Craig

foreword by James Paradis

"This book goes to the heart of what it means to learn and communicate in the fields of science and engineering. The students and teachers who appear in these cases engage us in the struggle to learn and teach. It's a book full of insights for teachers in STEM fields as well as teachers of technical/scientific communication. And this book's insights are not only for those at elite schools like MIT but anywhere students struggle to make meaning in scientific fields."
— David R. Russell, English Department, Iowa State University

272 pp., 9 illus., $35 cloth

$p_2 = \left[\frac{\lambda + \mu}{\mu}\right]\left[\frac{\lambda}{\mu}\right] p_0$

$n = 2;$ again (from

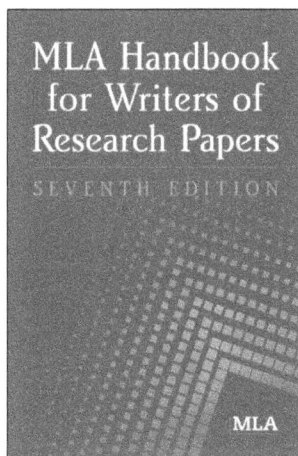

ESSAY

Teaching by Indirection

Bob Mayberry

> *Someone is watching me. I keep walking. The campus
> seems strangely empty for the middle of the day. The
> muscles in the back of my neck are taut, my pace
> quickens, my stride shortens as I turn up the brick path
> that leads between the cement columns guarding the
> heavy glass and metal doors to Fransden Humanities.
> Behind me, across the narrow campus street, stands the
> smaller, newer business building, a flat-topped, shoe-box
> shaped edifice with a row of windows looking at those
> pillars of humanity. Someone's out there, behind those
> windows, watching me, I know it, their eyes staring
> through me, burning a hole in the small of my back,
> burning through the muscle and bone and down through
> my intestines—because now they're on top of the roof of
> the business building, looking down on me—tearing a
> hole through to my groin—and suddenly it comes to me
> who they are, and I turn to face them: the men on my
> draft board and the men on the Board of Regents,
> combined, as if they were schizophrenics playing two
> discrete roles in my life, nameless faces to me, but
> recognizable in their gray and blue suits, short hair and
> clean-shaven faces, featureless except for the intensity of
> their stares. It's not hate I see on their faces, I see
> nothing, men without feelings, men staring coldly at an
> aberrant cog in their machine, a fly in their ointment. They
> pick up rifles with huge scopes, the hole in my guts is cold
> where the wind blows through, and I spin in panic toward
> the doors, up the steps and between the arms of the
> columns, I fly for the doors*

• • •

This dream haunted me during my junior year in college, 1971. Nixon had eliminated student deferrals, instituted a draft lottery, and bombed Cambodia. Peace rallies were daily events on college campuses. I was preparing to battle the draft board over my conscientious objector application when the Board of Regents fired my English professor, Paul Adamian, for "participa-

Composition Studies 38.1 (2010) / ISSN 1534-9322

tion in anti-Vietnam war activities." The dream first woke me the night after hearing the news that three students had been shot by National Guardsmen at Kent State; it still occasionally jars me from my sleep decades later.

In slow motion, like a too-brightly lit sequence from a violent film, I see myself approach the humanities building. I'm conscious of myself both as actor and audience, the script is clear to me now, I know how the story ends, but I watch fascinated and horrified, like a patient awake during the operation. A single bullet rips through the small of my back, shattering my spinal cord and disconnecting all feeling from my legs, tearing the tissue and intestinal tubing, exploding out through my balls and penis, spilling blood and tissue against the glass of the door while I fall slowly toward the glass panel in the middle of the door, my hands catching my fall and turning white under the weight of my body, and I see—just before my face slams against the glass—my English professor and advisor, Paul Adamian, standing before me in the hall of the humanities building, his face filled with pain. I hit the door and black out.

• • •

Fall 1969, poetry class:

Uncle Paul weaves on

That line, that class, that man: stuck in my brain for forty years.

Uncle Paul weaves on
complicating simplicity

I majored in English because of Paul Adamian, became a teacher in no small part because of Paul, became the kind of teacher I am in large part because of him, yet I argued with him from the first day of our first class— and I loathed the smell of his cigarettes.

nervously puffing on
his packaged Viceroys

Remember 1969, before smoking was banned from classrooms? How I choked on the smell of the unfiltered cigarettes he chain-smoked through every class I took from him: freshman comp, intro to literary study, intro to poetry, British lit survey, ethnic lit. Yet somehow he taught me, changed me, in profound ways, in spite of his damn cigarettes. If I can figure out how, I'll understand something of how I learn and why I teach the way I do.

The story begins in my very first college classroom, winds its way through a smoke-filled poetry class

> around my desk
> swirls Marlboro Country

and culminates in the recurring nightmare at the doors of Fransden Humanities, where English classes were typically held. But the story doesn't end there, it doesn't end at all: Paul continues to haunt me, in part because he disappeared from my life and from academe, and I've been looking for him since.

I walked into my Monday morning freshman composition class in September of 1968. A thin man with graying hair paced across the front of the room smoking a cigarette. His eyes were on the floor, his thoughts somewhere else. His steps were short, quick. He'd stop momentarily when he reached the blackboard or windows, then turn sharply, exhale smoke and resume pacing. His right hand was always busy with the cigarette.

Between puffs he chewed his lip. He went through two cigarettes before class started, and he never stopped smoking: not when class began, not when it ended, not for fifteen weeks, nor for the three years I knew him.

> Uncle Paul weaves on

I didn't call him Uncle Paul until later, after he had weaved his way into my thinking, complicating every answer I thought I knew, and smoking up a storm. He was the most nervous teacher I've ever known. And even his nervousness was a gift to me, of sorts. Years later, when I stood in front of my first class as a teaching assistant, a freshman comp class at the same university, I told my students about my first images of Paul Adamian. I imitated his nervous pacing, mimed puffing a cigarette, even stared out the windows like he used to do. I poured my own anxieties on my first day teaching into this little parody, and the class—out of the generosity of youth or their own nervousness, I'll never know—laughed. I've used Paul in that way many times since, to ease myself and my students past those first few moments of discomfort in a new class.

Paul never seemed to get comfortable in front of our class that first semester. At midterm he asked us to answer a series of true-false questions about his teaching, questions like: Did he communicate clearly? Did he speak too fast? Were we involved in class discussions? The last question I remember verbatim: "Do I seem nervous to you?" What a question to ask a freshman! Of course he seemed nervous to me, but if I told him that he'd only become more nervous, wouldn't he? I wondered, still wonder, what he made of those answers. A few years later teacher evaluations became standard issue in most classrooms, though usually conducted at the end of the term. Paul's evaluation questions were more personal—he'd written them up himself instead of using a standardized form—and more pertinent: since they came at midterm, and since the prof. was voluntarily asking for this information, we knew our answers would affect the remainder of the course. From time to time I recall how important Paul's questions made me feel—he wants to know what I think!—and, so, around midterm I ask my students to tell me how our class is progressing. Another unintended gift from Uncle Paul.

I'm not sure I fully appreciated Paul Adamian that first semester, but I knew, even then, I was hooked. I never missed a class, came prepared to argue anything with him, read and reread my assignments to arm myself with arguments to counter his. I fought his liberal ideas tooth and nail, sounded like the archest conservative in the class, though at home I argued the liberal line with my father and hung around with my radical friends in the antiwar movement. What was going on? Something in Paul's teaching style persuaded me that the best way to learn from this man was to argue with him. I'm not suggesting that was a conscious decision, though I knew full well I was playing a role in class to bait Paul, making the most extreme conservative statements to see how he'd respond. Maybe I was using him to shore up my own arguments with my father and with society in general, learning the liberal line by posing as a conservative.

Perhaps I was hungry for his attention, perhaps I was testing my new educational environment, but I began to rebel against Paul's assignments. They were typical "analyze this reading" assignments. We were given an essay or book to read and discuss in class. After a couple days of discussion, Paul would say something like, "So now write an essay on the reading." He seemed embarrassed to even ask. He rarely elaborated on his assignments, which angered and confused many in the class. (I learned a great deal in opposition to Paul, not just from his strengths but his weaknesses, from the unintentional as well as intentional lessons. And because of what I learned, I am more explicit and deliberate than Paul about creating and conveying to students a context for writing assignments.)

Late in the semester, I decided to challenge his vague assignments. If Paul wasn't going to specify what he wanted, I'd seize the opportunity to write what I wanted. Ignoring entirely one of Paul's assignments, I chose to respond to a lyric by Paul Simon:

> time time time
> see what's become of me
> while I looked around
> for my possibilities
> I was so hard to please

Simon's song drips with irony now, forty years later, but at the time Simon articulated a generation's doubts about a very uncertain future.

> hang onto your hopes my friend
> that's an easy thing to say
> but if your hopes should pass away
> then simply pretend
> that you can build them again

Simon wrote the song as he neared thirty years of age, the final gasp of youth ("Never trust anyone over thirty"), but I assumed he was my age, knew what a college freshman was feeling and spoke directly to me:

> look around, grass is high, fields are ripe
> it's the springtime of my life

The paper, which I would quote here if it hadn't gotten lost during one of the many moves of my academic career, was the first I wrote in which the pronoun "I" took center stage. Like many of my students today, I'd been discouraged during high school from using "I" in class papers. I'd certainly never written a paper about myself, particularly about vague perceptions, adolescent guilt, the sense I was wasting my life, not doing anything productive.

I remember waiting anxiously for Paul to return the paper. I have no idea what grade I got, but I'll remember to my dying day the one brief substantive comment at the end of the paper, written in brown ink: "More of these personal connections." More? I was flabbergasted. In one phrase Uncle Paul had overthrown my high school education, undermined my rebellion and made me want to write for him. More, indeed.

Paul got his wish, and more: over the next two years, I took five classes from Professor Adamian, wrote dozens of papers for him—most very personal, a couple written in verse rather than prose—changed my major to English and appointed him my advisor. And now, forty years later, I'm writing about Paul rather than for him.

The semester after the comp class and the Paul Simon paper, I enrolled for two classes with Uncle Paul, including a poetry class which inspired a poem about Paul's teaching and smoking. His pedagogy frustrated me at the time, though now I emulate it. I think of it as teaching by indirection, though at the time I wondered what the hell he was doing.

Paul invited the class to choose which poets we wanted to read for the semester. He asked each of us to prepare a paper or presentation on a poet or poem, and it was our ideas and analyses that shaped class, not his. This was the first time I'd encountered a teacher who didn't tell the class what the right or best or preferred interpretation of a story or poem was. Paul remained strangely silent while we discussed the poems, and then he would begin to talk about our interpretations, questioning them and at the same time exploring them more deeply than we had. He arrived at no conclusions, offered no answers, gave no tests. He just complicated our thinking, all the while smoking his damn cigarettes. In fact, most of the class smoked, or they seem to in the dimly-lit, smoke-filled, air-choked room of my memory.

> around my desk
> swirls Marlboro Country
> Camels stampeding
> up my nostrils

I was looking for a way to tell Paul how frustrated I was not having him toargue with and how sick I was of the smoke, when he assigned a poem by Gary Snyder, "Marin-An."

> sun breaks over the eucalyptus
> grove below the wet pasture,
> water's about hot,
> I sit in the open window
> & roll a smoke.
> . . .
> a soft continuous roar
> comes out of the far valley
> of the six-lane highway–thousands

and thousands of cars
driving men to work.

Snyder's poem spoke to me and my dissatisfaction with class. The speaker seems removed from what is happening around him; he wants out of it, the traffic, the noise, the urban life. So he rolls his own. I thought of Paul, so removed that semester. I wondered if he wanted out of it, if he too were rolling his own. A poem began to take shape in my mind as a question to him, and a complaint. I started it by referring to Snyder's text

on the page
the poet's truth:
he rolls his own

and linked it to my frustrations in class. I was doing what Paul had encouraged me to do the previous semester in freshman comp: personally investing myself in my writing. I got to class early one day and wrote the poem on the board:

on the page
the poet's truth:
he rolls his own

around my desk
swirls Marlboro Country
Camels stampeding
up my nostrils

Uncle Paul weaves on
complicating simplicity
nervously puffing on
his packaged Viceroys
Why don't you roll your own?

Students wandered in, read the poem, asked each other if it was an assignment, wondered who had written it. I said nothing. Paul came in, read it aloud to the class, smiled, and wrote the closing pair of lines to the poem:

I do
at home

That was flattery. That was empowerment. My writing treated as a text in a course, and Paul did it a decade or more before any of it was in vogue, before "empowerment" became a buzz word, before we even had a vocabulary to describe what he did.

That class period turned the semester around for me. Paul weaved me into the Snyder poem, and out of that I rolled my own poem. His pedagogy of indirection suckered me into authoring my own education; he conned me into joining the conversation of literature, and in so doing made an English major of me. And what were his great teaching techniques? Patience, invitation, reception.

He did so little, and I learned so much. His was the art of unteaching.

• • •

Paul was fired a year after that poetry class. The Regents wanted a scapegoat to blame for the increased frequency of student protests. (As if the Vietnam War wasn't reason enough!) When students and faculty halted the Governor's motorcade during an ROTC awards ceremony, held only days after the shootings at Kent State, the Regents launched a witch hunt. They scoured press photos until they could identify one faculty member among the protesters: Paul Adamian. They blamed him for the student protests and ordered the university president to bring charges against him, but when the appointed faculty committee recommended censure the Regents fired Paul anyway, ignoring the student testimonials to his extraordinary teaching — as well as the fact that the Regents had just conferred tenure upon Paul a year before.

The Regents pursued their case against Paul all semester long. I watched his spirit and enthusiasm, his love of literature and care for students erode in the face of the Regents' charges and unrelenting accusations in the local press. By the end of the term, when the Regents met to formally dismiss Paul, he was a changed man bearing little resemblance to the teacher I'd known and loved. Bitter and broken, he stood against the back wall during that meeting, his spine curved at the neck, head dipped downward, one hand in the pocket of that awful nylon wind breaker he always wore, the other holding a cigarette against his hip, his eyes darting among the faces of the Regents, one at a time, counting them, assessing them, more aware of his fate than any of the students who'd come to support him, hopeful in our idealistic naiveté that our testimonials would sway the Regents.

During that public hearing I studied Paul, trying to see in his hawk-like profile or the intensity of his eyes the teacher who'd changed my life. He fiddled constantly with the cigarette between his fingers, reminding me of that first day in freshman composition, how nervous he was, puffing on his Viceroys and beginning every sentence with a lengthy "uhh." I remembered that before our class got to know him, before we began calling him Uncle Paul, we used to count the number of uhhs he uttered during each hour and wager our pocket change on the outcome. But we soon forgot such silliness when Paul began challenging our comfortable habits of thought. Every time I'd offer a generalization he'd counter with "Whadda you mean exactly?" To each of my pat answers he'd say, "Yeah, but do you believe that? Is it true? Is it really important?" Paul's questions pushed me to clarify my own beliefs, and when I proudly announced that something was unjust or immoral, he'd look at me with that smirk of his and ask, "So what are you gonna do about it?"

I remembered that midway through that first semester, Paul called me at home to say he wasn't coming to class that morning. Thanks for telling me, I said, it'll save me the drive across town.

No, he said, he wasn't canceling class, he wanted me to lead the discussion.

But, I said.

You can do it, he said.

But, I said.

Discussion hasn't been going too well, he said, and I want to find out if it's me, if students aren't talking because of me, because I'm too overbearing or something.

He sounded pained, troubled that he didn't know how to improve the quality of class discussions. How often have I had a teacher so intent on improving discussions that he would absent himself? I told him I didn't know how to teach, and he assured me I would do just fine. Just let them talk, he said, see what happens and then come by my office and let me know.

So I did. The discussion was, as he suspected, livelier than usual, through no effort of mine. When I reported to him after class, he said, Maybe you're just a better teacher. And for a moment I thought maybe I could be. But no, I realized when my swollen head subsided, I could never care as much as he did.

I think it was at that point Paul began to experiment with different classroom strategies—including, a year later, teaching the poetry class by indirection. He was searching for any means at his disposal to get students involved.

Paul didn't have to lecture about his beliefs, he let his actions speak for him—in the classroom and in the world. He was the most principled and conscientious man I'd known, and his integrity cost him his career.

At the end of that public hearing a year later, the Regents exited the room of students and faculty and produced, in less than thirty minutes, a twenty page document terminating Professor Adamian. The hearing was a sham. The document had been prepared days or weeks ahead of time. The Regents never listened to a word we said. And Paul never taught again.

· · ·

> *Find your enemy. When you know*
> *what you're against you have taken*
> *the first step to discovering what*
> *you're for.*
> —Salman Rushdie

The specter of Uncle Paul haunted me for thirty years. I'd neither seen nor spoken to him, though I went searching for him once in Northern California, where mutual friends said he lived awhile. No luck. I've written letters to him, unsent, and stories about him, unfinished, as my own career has wandered from one university to another. Each time I step nervously into a new class, I'm reminded of his chain-smoking and pacing in front of class. Whenever my own teaching seems stuck or routine, I remember his passion for getting students involved.

Paul taught me more than the lessons about literature I've long since forgotten, more even than the technique of teaching by indirection. He taught me something important about the profession I would later enter: he taught me who the enemies were.

Since completing my PhD in 1979, I've held various teaching positions at ten different institutions—part-time, full-time non tenure-track, and four tenure-track jobs. One colleague calls me a vagabond scholar. Others wonder what I've been running from. The answer's obvious: Paul's fate. I watched the Regents destroy a tenured professor's career, so I assiduously avoided tenure for the next quarter century. More than avoided, I feared it, afraid I might become like the timid members of Paul's department who, in response to his firing, were too frightened for their own positions

(Paul wasn't the only English prof involved in antiwar protests) to do anything more than write a letter requesting the Regents reconsider their decision. I promised myself never to get so comfortable that I wouldn't be willing to campaign actively against injustice, be it war or the firing of a colleague.

And so I learned from Paul who the enemies of good teaching are: the enemies within, like complacency and fear, as well as the enemies without, politically motivated Regents and administrators, even the institution itself.

One way to avoid becoming complacent was to remain untenured. But that didn't protect me from being fired from a lecturer position I held for five years—not for political protest but for pedagogical presumption.

Fourteen lecturers were hired by the University of Nevada, Las Vegas, English department in the early 1990s to teach the required composition courses. When we began working with the comp director to change the freshman course, chiefly by introducing process pedagogy into our classes, the literature faculty objected. They introduced resolutions at department meetings (where lecturers were barred from voting) designed to force us to conform to their notions of how writing should be taught. One lit prof. asserted the comp program should "go back to the way it was twenty years ago." Another wanted "more formulaic writing." They asserted that peer editing "was a waste of time"; so was encouraging students to talk to each other. By the end of the meeting, they had passed a new departmental policy requiring every error in every student draft to be marked in red ink. So much for the process. One senior faculty member awoke long enough from his afternoon nap to hear the reading of the motion, panicked, and asked if he was expected to do that in his classes. His colleagues chuckled; of course not, the policy applied only to comp teachers.

I chuckle about these events now, but at the time I seethed. Even a couple years later, when I'd escaped UNLV and landed myself a tenure-track job in a very teacher-supportive college in Alaska, I found writing about the events very difficult. I anguished over how to tell the story. Just "getting even" wasn't enough, I wanted to shout out loud, "These are the enemies of good teaching; this is what we must avoid becoming." To tell my story I developed a metaphor of closed and open doors (see my article "Opening Doors"). Prior to the literature faculty's intrusion into composition pedagogy, I'd always left my classroom door open while teaching, in large part because the tiny, windowless classrooms were stultifying, casket-like. But after the infamous meeting I closed the door every time I walked into class.

When I arrived in Alaska, I not only discovered classrooms with windows (and what a view!—jagged, snowcapped mountains or open ocean in every direction), but I rediscovered the pleasures of teaching with the classroom door wide open. What a treat it was to have colleagues wave as they passed, to hear students speak to each other through the open door, to invite their friends and family in to join us. My teaching doors have remained open since.

My partner Denise Stephenson pointed out to me the connection between the doors at UNLV and those in my dream about Uncle Paul and the Regent/Draft Board snipers. Why hadn't I seen that? For years, I struggled against closed doors—the locked glass doors in my dream, the doors I slammed shut at UNLV, the doors of tenure. In spite of the many years I studied in classrooms with open doors and the few years when I could teach without fear myself, it's the doors closed to innovative teaching that have defined my own academic struggles. In knowing the enemy, as Rushdie says, I have learned what I stand for.

When I finally faced tenure a couple years ago, I realized the time had come to put my fears behind me, to put to rest the nightmare that has haunted my academic career. I needed to find Uncle Paul.

By a strange circuit of coincidences, a doctoral student was researching the history of Paul Adamian's firing at the same time I began work on this essay. He happened to interview an old friend of mine, who then contacted me. We wondered what had happened to Paul. My friend eventually found Paul's phone number and emailed it to me.

I was apprehensive about how to bridge the years since we'd last spoken. Whole lifetimes had intervened. I knew only the young Professor Adamian; what had he become? Would he remember me? Or would he want to forget his academic past? Would he dismiss me for becoming an English prof? And how would he feel about this chapter I've written about him?

At first the voice on the other end of the line was unrecognizable, then he laughed and I had a sudden image of his face in class, in the years before the hearings and firing, his eyes dancing with laughter, the deep lines of his face rising into a toothy smile, as the small explosions of a smoker's halflaugh, half-hack issued from his throat. He laughed a lot back then and it was reassuring to hear it again thirty years later. He'd made a new career for himself outside the academy, as a fisherman. An aptly metaphoric trade for a martyred teacher, I thought.

We spoke for half an hour, more about the present than the past, and while part of me wants to lament the loss of a great teacher, I realize that Uncle Paul continues to influence students—my students—because he has so profoundly influenced me, sometimes directly and intentionally in the classroom, but more often indirectly, and probably without knowing it, simply by being an example.

Uncle Paul untaught me to unteach, and I've been ungrateful ever since. So let me undo my past omissions, and let this chapter be an expression of my gratitude to my first unteacher.

Sources

Mayberry, Bob. "Opening Doors." *Composition Studies* 23.1, 1995: 78-93. Print.

Rushdie, Salman. *The Ground Beneath Her Feet.* New York: Holt, 1999. Print

Simon, Paul. "A Hazy Shade of Winter." *Bookends.* BMI, 1968. CD

Snyder, Gary. "Marin-An." *Many Californias: literature from the Golden State.* Ed. Gerald Haslam. U of Nevada P 1999. 172-173. Print.

Active Voices: Composing a Rhetoric of Social Movements, edited by Sharon McKenzie Stevens and Patricia Malesh. Albany: State University of New York Press, 2009. 263 pp.

Reviewed by Diana Yıldız, Georgia State University

A guidepost at the intersection of sociology, political science, communication studies, and rhetoric and composition, *Active Voices: Composing a Rhetoric of Social Movements* purports to redefine the scholarship of social movements. In their introductory essay, editors Sharon McKenzie Stevens and Patricia Malesh provide a view of the intellectual zeitgeist of social movement studies in the U.S., a milieu complicated by a blurring of the demarcations between private and public spheres. To illustrate this blurring, Stevens and Malesh cite the mining of user profiles by Internet companies, the imprisonment of journalists for insisting upon the anonymity of their sources, the warrantless wiretapping instituted by the Bush administration, and the surveillance of domestic advocacy groups. Once the disenfranchised made what was private public in order to shed light on wrongs, but no longer, the editors contend. Rather, dominant institutions of American society have broken down and redfined the privacy of no-longer private citizens.

Responding to this sea change in public discourse, the editors seek to distinguish their volume by resituating rhetoric, particularly in regard to social change, as "the study of who is trying to do what to whom, with particular emphasis on how and why they are doing it" (7). Absent from this nebulous, unsettling definition is any reference to language, image, or other form of communication. This definition portrays merely the agonistic nature of rhetoric, including no acknowledgement of how rhetoric can and does effect positive social changes.

Despite this problematic theoretical underpinning, the editors provide a useful overview of trends in social movement theories, noting these stages of focus: collective behavior or structural strain, resource mobilization paradigm, framing processes, and new social movement studies (NSMs). Although social movement research traditionally has been performed by sociologists and scholars in Communication Studies, Stevens and Malesh champion rhetoricians as being especially well-suited to the "meta-inquiry" of social movement studies, particularly since it is "grounded in persuasion, discourse, and interaction" (11). Furthermore, through their pedagogical focus, Composition scholars can enact civic praxis because the classroom "embodies the dialectical relationship between theory and practice—theory informs practice, practice restructures theory, and theory crafts future" (15). Even though the studies within the book are primarily inductive, the book itself has a deductive structure, beginning with theories and ending with specific pedagogies.

Part I of *Active Voices*, "A New Rhetoric for Social Change: Theories," contains two essays. In "Vernacular Rhetoric and Social Movements: Performances of Resistance in the Rhetoric of the Everyday," Gerard Hauser and erin daina mcclellan propose that social movement studies should focus less on charismatic leaders and more on rank-and-file members. To this end, the authors use Hauser's term vernacular rhetoric, which they explain exemplifies Kenneth Burke's consideration of all of human symbolic action as rhetorical. Forms of vernacular rhetoric include letters to the editor, graffiti, music, and bodily displays, eliding the line between discursive and nondiscursive practices. Hauser and mcclellan's essay proves to be one of the best-researched and most engaging pieces in the volume.

The next essay, "Dreaming to Change Our Situation: Reconfiguring the Exigence for Student Writing," by Sharon McKenzie Stevens, is comparatively slight. Stevens outlines theories about the rhetorical situation by figures such as Lloyd Bitzer, Barbara Biesecker, and Jenny Edbauer, ultimately privileging Kenneth Burke's notion of identification to best explain how teachers and scholars can expand Bitzer's restrictive view of audience. Stevens concludes that teachers can help students break down the dichotomy of public and private by composing texts for an audience beyond the classroom (60). The most useful part of her essay is an analysis of several college writing handbooks, some of which equate the modes of discourse with "writing situations" (49-50). Another practical aspect provides a rough course outline exemplifying the principles of expansion Stevens promotes (60-63).

Part II of *Active Voices*, "Public Rhetorics: Analyses," contains rhetorical analyses of social movement texts. Moira K. Amado-Miller writes "Disorderly Women: Appropriating the Power Tools in Civic Discourses" to examine how feminists in the suffrage movement employed subversive uses of the classical rhetorical trope of *antistrephon*. Focusing on education as another arena of extensive social change, Brian Jackson and Thomas P. Miller trace the cause of the Progressive Education Association's failure. In "The Progressive Education Movement: A Case Study in Coalition Politics," Jackson and Miller explain that the PEA, which championed the theories of John Dewey, privileged the views of scientifically trained professionals in higher education at the cost of giving a voice to the emerging professional educators in public schools (95). Jackson and Miller's argument speaks to Hauser and mcclellan's promotion of vernacular rhetoric. Thomas Rosteck performs an engaging analysis of C. Wright Mills's use of the public letter in "Giving Voice to a Movement: Mills's 'Letter to the New Left' and the Potential of History." According to Rosteck, through tone and the use of first and second person pronouns, Mills creates two audiences: those in the nascent movement and those he wants to recruit into the movement. His clever use of the public letter, a liminal space between public and private, also allows him to create a flexible persona for himself. In this assertion, Rosteck's essay speaks to Stevens's reinscribing of audience in the rhetorical situation. Patricia Malesh performs a readable analysis in "Sharing Our Recipes: Vegan Conversion Narratives as Social Praxis." Drawing upon both narrative theory and social movement theory, Malesh identifies a rhetorical turn in ethos embodies in these tales: the narrator, once a mentee, becomes through the telling, a mentor for the audience. Her essay speaks to Amado-Miller's explication of how narratives shift power dynamics for the rhetor.

In Part III, "Changing Spaces for Learning: Actions," the focus of *Active Voices* turns to classroom practice and praxis. David Coogan's "Moving Students into Social Movements: Prison Reentry and the Research Paper" narrates the intellectual and emotional changes evident in his students resulting from their interaction with released prisoners trying to create a life outside bars. Throughout this essay is a subtle yet powerful argument for reexamining the perceptions and rhetoric surrounding prisoner rehabilitation. "Engaging Globalization through Local Community Activism: A Model for Activist Peda-gogical Practice" by Anne Marie Todd demonstrates how teaching community activism engages students: "Through participant observation of an activist group, students gain insight into the notion of civic responsibility from being themselves politically engaged" (175). While this statement may not seem profound, Todd nonetheless calls needed attention to an overlooked aspect of pedagogy: service learning. The final essay of this section, "'Creating Space' for Community: Radical Identities and Collective Praxis," shows the ways in which performative rhetoric can reify the material rhetoric that is often invis-ible to students. Mary Ann Cain describes a performance by the Three Rivers Jenbé Ensemble as embodying a "third space" in which discursive (symbolic) and extradiscursive (material) aspects of language and rhetoric can exist in harmony. She contrasts this "habitable space" with the "transient space" that represents the typical college classroom, but she does not offer a practical way to incorporate this performative/material rhetoric into pedagogy, a crucial weakness in an otherwise sound and well-researched piece.

In a response essay concluding the volume, William DeGenaro echoes the importance of rejecting the "cultural-material binary," a prevalent theme in this anthology (203-04). He makes several salient and insightful points in "Politics, Class and Social Movement People: Continuing the Conversa-tion." Fellow scholars, he urges, must forget neither the human face of social movements nor the necessary methods of ethnography and archival research that constitute ways to unearth the contributions of often-forgotten people. DeGenaro emphasizes that the shift in notions of public and private represents an integral part of social movements, which are increasingly characterized by their followers' identities. More significantly, DeGenaro observes that social movements are not just about identity, but have been also typically stratified by class, a marker that needs careful study due to "our current moment of transition" (204). In this transition, he explains, fiscally conservative elites have joined forces with socially conservative working-class people to form new movements on the political Right. The radical rhetoric of fundamentalist Christians and neoconservatives as well as the "curmudgeonly" rhetoric of liberals trying to protect entitlement programs have been neglected by largely progressive scholars of rhetoric, and DeGenaro justifiably points out this gaping hole in our field (201-03). DeGenaro posits the best ways to meet these new developments are rooted in creativity and coalition building, and we should rejoice that social movement scholarship is thriving.

DeGenaro's reflection on *Active Voices* honors the power of social movements and those who study them in effecting social change. Scholars and teachers of Composition and Rhetoric should read this book, certainly, but so too should Communication Studies scholars and teachers, as well as those in Anthropology, Sociology, and Political Science. The intersection of social movements and rhetoric encompasses not only the humanities and the social sciences, but also nearly every facet of academic and personal life.

Atlanta, GA

Teaching the New Writing: Technology, Change, and Assessment in the 21st Century Classroom. edited by Anne Herrington, Kevin Hodgson, and Charles Moran. Teachers College Press and the National Writing Project, 2009. 228 pages.

Reviewed by S. Morgan Gresham, University of South Florida St. Petersburg

What does writing in the 21st century look like? We know that it is often project-based. It includes blogs, digital books, podcasts, and hybrid compositions. It is collaboratively conceived and generated. Questions remain, however, about how classroom teachers implement and assess these multimodal texts. *Teaching the New Writing: Technology, Change, and Assessment in the 21st Century Classroom* attempts answers. With twelve chapters that provide three or four examples from each level, *Teaching the New Writing* captures the intersection of school-sponsored literacy practices and state-sponsored literacy assessments, providing an overview of many ways in which writing, technologies, and assessment practices come together in elementary, secondary, and post-secondary classrooms across the country. In the early 1990s, Charles Moran, one of the editors of *Teaching the New Writing*, argued that we need to stay aware of the seams of technology even as we shift and adapt to technologies so that we can locate the patterns of our usage and remain critical of how we shape the technology and it shapes us. Here, Moran, with co-editors Herrington and Hodgson, pushes readers to acknowledge how, despite the constant reshaping of technologies available to writing teachers, the practices of what we do as writing teachers remains the teaching of writing, broadly writ, as composition. In example classrooms, teachers demonstrate a critical awareness that the technologies need not dictate the compositions or the assessments of those compositions.

Serving as an overview, Herrington and Moran's chapter opens the collection by reminding readers of the evolution of computers' inclusion in the writing classroom and then defining the key terms of state-sponsored writing assessment practices such as Texas and Illinois' testing systems and Kentucky's portfolio system. The clear point of contrast between the school-sponsored literacy practices and the state-sponsored assessments is the absence of multimodality in state-sponsored assessment, even in more progressive portfolio assessments. The different roles assessment plays vary according to the definitions the chapter authors assign to assessment. What transcends these multiple definitions is adaptability in the classroom. In "Collaborative Digital Writing," Bledsoe makes a distinction between assessment and evaluation, arguing that although these terms are often used interchangeably, he defines "assessment" as a classroom activity that teachers use to "guide their instruction" (48) whereas evaluation is the process of "giving value to a body of work . . . with a target audience in mind" (49), and he goes on to point out that "evaluation is most powerful . . . when it doesn't come from the teacher" (50). If we read evaluation in the context of feedback response, then there is a clear connection between Bledsoe's distinctions about assessment and evaluation and the valuation of collaboration that spans the sections.

Part 1, "Beginning in Elementary and Middle School," establishes the functionality of computer technologies to enable beginning and developing writers to create multimodal texts that mimic the real world texts they encounter outside the classroom. Marva Solomon in chapter 2 describes her work with struggling readers and English Language Learners as they develop web sites with multiple pages that include images and graphics alongside student researched and generated text. Students connected with one another and their creations as they wrote. Solomon writes, "Online writing is not quiet . . . All the children had strong physical reactions to the multimodal elements they added to their pages" (36), and as I have been watching my own students develop video and mixed media productions, I recognize the truth in Solomon's statement. It echoes Moran's initial reminder that for these students, this technology is not seamless, and therefore carries a newness that is immediate, visceral, and engaging. Further, this part underscores the social nature of computer-mediated writing by describing collaboratively written stories by fourth graders ("Collaborative Digital Writing") and sixth graders ("Digital Picture Books") in addition to Solomon's active learners. In these chapters, we see communities of writers being established based around their shared goals of communication, development and elaboration of text and graphics.

The focus on collaborative learning continues in part 2, "Continuing in the Secondary Grades," with a focus on outside audiences reached through blogs, videos, and multimedia presentations. With older, more experienced student writers, instructors explore a greater diversity of technologies. Paul Allison helps his high school students to become bloggers by asking them to find something they are passionate about and then to share what they know with others (80). Drawing out the composing process, students create blogs and develop social networks based on their interests. Jeffrey Schwartz describes how ninth graders use Word, iTunes, Garage Band, and iMovie to interpret poetry through video in "Poetry Fusion: Integrating Video, Verbal, and Audio Texts." Kentucky's state-mandated student portfolios take on new life through student-directed senior project presentations in "Senior Boards: Multimedia Presentations." Created as a supplement to the scripted assignments and assessments of the state portfolios that, interestingly, do not allow group entries or account for pictures, tables, charts and graphs, the student board presentations prove a catalyst for continued research, conversation, and computer innovations. Finally, we are reminded that multimodality is not limited to the visual through Reed and Hicks' examination of audio blogs in speech classes. In this case, audience takes the fore as students develop podcasts following NPR's "This I Believe" format with a goal of creating for students "a meaningful online experience" (126) as mandated by the Michigan Department of Education. The authors describe these speech students' awareness of audience as their materials receive responses from peers, parents, and other citizens of the World Wide Web.

Part 3, entitled "Bridging to the College Years," continues the progression of technology integration first by examining more closely the collaborative writing of scientists. Computer technologies and multimodality change scientific writing for high school and college student writers. Poe and Radkowski Opperman's effort in "Scientific Writing and Technological Change" foregrounds collaboration as a technology that serves both development and assessment purposes for student writers in scientific writing classes. Collaboration ties with identity as Kittle narrates the evolution of his students' experiments with literacy narratives "Student Engagement and Multimodality." Kittle argues that video and still images dramatically shift the readers' perspectives on the narratives and with this shift comes a new approach to the assessment of the projects, in which Kittle creates MP3 responses in addition to the scoring rubric.

In his earlier work, Moran seems to remind us that we should occasionally state what is often unstated, and in closing the text, the editors write, "Our chapter-authors are modeling for their students the values we admire: doing a project for its own sake, for one's own self-satisfaction, and for an audience of peers and significant adults; using one's imagination and intellect to compose texts that engage, inform, and persuade other people" (207). Alongside those stated values, a critical awareness of the variable nature of writing lies at the heart of this collection. In these moments of classroom practices, we see the following:

- Writing at its best is a process that is collaborative, multimodal, and adaptive.
- Writing teachers teach a series of skills as well as approaches.
- Feedback from a range of audiences—including peers and teachers— is crucial to effective communication.
- Assessment is a changing technology inasmuch as computer technologies are evolving.
- Writing teachers who incorporate computer technologies continue to experiment and adapt both with project assignments and assessments/evaluations even in the face of high-stakes outside assessments.

Although these chapters are mostly success stories for teacher and students alike, difficulties encountered by both across the grades include limited access to computers and computer programs in and out of school, loss of work caused by technology failures, and unfamiliarity with multimodal composing tools and software. However, despite instructors' initial trepidation about working with and assessing multimodal compositions, all accounts describe successful assessment or evaluation practices within the confines of the classrooms in which the assignments are developed. In addition to assignment ideas and descriptions, teachers will find in *Teaching the New Writing* an assortment of teaching tools and scoring guides including those for digital picture book projects (67), video poetry assignments (103), critiques of peer reports (157), multimodal documents (172), and hybrid essays (194).

A particular appeal of this text is its landscape approach to writing. We are fortunate to bear witness to a multimodal curriculum in which we can envision the students' development across platforms, genres, and time. Repeatedly we hear students' positive response to the innovative and technology-rich projects they encounter throughout the collection. It is not difficult to imagine those 2nd graders Solomon describes as they might encounter Allison's blogging class or Reed and Hicks' speech class to arrive finally in Smith's college writing course. These students may well deliver on the promise that Smith alludes to when he describes the pervasive *text*uality of his current students' multimodal compositions "so that we can move beyond our greatest strength and weakness—a reliance upon print media to make meaning" (191).

St. Petersburg, FL

Work Cited

Moran, Charles. "We Write, but Do We Read?" *Computers and Composition* 8.3 (1991): 51-62. Print.

Ecosee: Image, Rhetoric, Nature, edited by Sidney I. Dobrin and Sean Morey. Albany State University of New York Press, 2009. 327 pp.

Reviewed by Alexis E. Ramsey, Eckerd College

Ecosee: Image, Rhetoric, Nature, edited by Sidney I. Dobrin and Sean Morey, acts as a continuation of the rhetorical analysis of environmental and ecological issues initiated by *Ecospeak: Rhetoric and Environmental Politics in America,* edited by M. Jimmie Killingsworth and Jaqueline S. Palmer. Whereas *Ecospeak* looked at the interplay among language, thought, and environmental action, *Ecosee* explores the role of the image in environmental discourses. Specifically, *Ecosee* "considers the role of visual rhetoric, picture theory, semiotics, and other image-based studies in understanding the construction and contestation of space, place, nature, environment, and ecology" (2). The aim of *Ecosee* is three-fold: to teach people how to read environmentally-based images; second, to help them consider the production process for these images; and third, to inspire readers to begin making images of their own. As Sean Moyer writes in chapter one "A Rhetorical Look at Ecosee," "theories of ecosee should help individuals recognize the conventional rhetorical devices and their intended effects, who can therefore accept or reject those meanings, or, once recognized, construct their own images of nature" (43). Indeed, the difficulty with theories of ecosee, according to Moyer, is getting "people to perceive, to pay attention to the billboards along the highway" (45) and then moving from perception to practice. Thus, the book is concerned with both the theory and praxis of visual environmental rhetoric.

Ecosee is divided into four parts: "How we See"; "Seeing Animals"; "Seeing Landscapes and Seascapes"; and "Seeing in Space and Time." Yet, as the editors make clear and as the volume mimics, ecosee, as a theory and as a text, is very much about interplay—the interplay of images and text, of images and environments, of images with each other, and of environmental rhetoric with other disciplinary approaches. Indeed, the first section considers the varying ways that we read and respond to environmental images. Following Moyer's chapter detailing ecosee as a rhetorical theory, the second chapter looks at ecopornography and the parallels between human-based pornography and nature-based photography. The third chapter focuses on art historians and calls for them to approach images from a rhetorical perspective. The final two chapters in the section examine two visual constructions of nature: field guides to birds and the art of Eduardo Kac.

The interplay inherent in the book continues into section two as contributors question the ethics of representing animals or non-human subjects and the role of production in these images. For example, Steve Baker's "They're There, and That's How We're Seeing It: Olly and Suzi in the Antarctic" traces the exploratory working methods of artists Olly and Suzi whose artistic process emphasizes "being there" or an attentiveness to their subject matter. While Olly and Suzi do not think it is their place to theorize their practice, Baker does explore the embodiedness underlying their work, particularly because they literally travel to the animals, drawing their subjects in the moment of observation. In doing so, Baker contends, Olly and Suzi help to disrupt the way humans tend to look at animals. The animals, alongside the artists, become part of a chain of ecological interdependence. The two other chapters in the section, Cary Wolfe's chapter comparing the work of artists Sue Coe and Eduardo Kac and Eleanor Morgan's chapter on visiting aquariums, question the role of the observer. As Morgan asks, "how do we look at nature?" And, by extension, how does that looking transform nature?

The third section of the book examines the politics of representation when applied to diverse environments and with diverse media, including film, with Pat Brereton's chapter offering an ecological reading of farming as represented in Irish cinema and Teresa E.P. Delfin's chapter on third world landscape photography. In "That's Not a Reef. Now *That's* a Reef: A Century of (Re)Placing the Great Barrier Reef," Kathryn Ferguson argues that photographic depictions of the Great Barrier Reef are creating skewed perceptions about the Reef by creating what she calls a "virtual reef" because the Reef is "in the process of being entirely replaced by its own image . . .What we are seeing . . . is all too often not the reef at all [but] a molded and marketed commodity" (226). In other words, images of the Great Barrier Reef are eclipsing the actual reef, which leads to unrealistic expectations about the reef and, in turn, causes a conundrum for reef conservation efforts. At issue is the fact that much of the reef no longer looks like its pictures, filled instead with bleached coral, anchor damage, and dead fish. Yet the efforts to save the reef are based on images that always refer to something earlier, to an origin that no longer exists. The question is thus two-fold: do we save the reef because of its "beauty," or do we save the reef because so much of it is in peril? In an interesting twist, Ferguson ends her chapter by debating the use of pictures in her chapter, asking her readers: Did you expect images? Did you look for them first before reading? What if the pictures showed the "non-pretty" sides of the reef? This direct address to the reader emphasizes the role of images in environmental rhetoric, because, to be honest, yes, I was expecting pictures of the reef.

This conundrum of visual representation continues in the final section of the book with chapters exploring the digital, inclusive environment of the video game *Civilization* along with two chapters examining the role of photography in social action. Quinn R. Gorman's "Evading Capture: The Productive Resistance of Photography in Environmental Representation" argues that photography may be the best medium for a "representational ethics that resists the very *possibility* of a complete capture of the natural" (242, italics in original). Photography, according to Gorman, and in particular environmental photography, can be both realistic and socially constructed; it need not be considered in an either/or light. Yet, says Gorman, even more important is that the photograph can offer a form of environmental motivation through either animation or a visceral response.

The power of photography is reiterated in "Seeing the Climate: The Problematic Status of Visual Evidence in Climate Change Campaigning" by Julie Doyle. She argues that the visual is so privileged in environmental communication that such communication can be stymied without images. Indeed, she points out that the argument for climate change did not gain widespread attention until it could be "witnessed" with and by images of melting glaciers. The problem, says Doyle, is that such dependence does not allow the projection of action into the future. We can document what has happened, but we cannot use visuals to forecast what will happen. There is a temporal value to the evidentiary force of a photograph.

In the Afterword, M. Jimmie Killingsworth and Jaqueline S. Palmer (editors of *Ecospeak*) laud the scholarly attention the authors pay to images, while noting that the work represented in the volume is just the beginning of environmental visual studies. One point they make is that, as scholars, we need to reconsider rhetorical theory in light of insights offered by the study of the visual and ecological imagination. By moving beyond reductive readings of images, we can start to appreciate that the effect of images is not inherent but is dependent on the creators and readers of the images. Thus, more than "looking" or "watching," we need "to attend"(302) to the image; we must be involved. This call to experience the photograph also emphasizes another tenet of ecosee—that it often functions best at the local level, attending to local concerns to communicate environmental messages and issues. Thus, the concept of ecosee as extended in the volume works to move beyond mass-mediated imagery. Understanding that much of our interaction with nature is inherently visual (6), the authors within *Ecosee* suggest that the more we understand this relationship, the more persuasively we can communicate with these visuals and the more we can begin to critique that which we see, asking not only "what is there?" but "what is left out" and "how can I add to what is shown?" And it is with this last question where *Ecosee* struggles. While ostensibly one of the aims of this text, few authors offer much guidance in the rhetoric of production. Certainly the authors involved do an excellent job in communicating the importance of visuals in environmental conversations and working toward the formation of a visual rhetoric, but they focus more on critiques of what has been made, published, and discussed than they do the actual process of converting attitudes and ideas into visual mediums. That said, *Ecosee* is a timely and valuable book especially as we are daily confronted with the "greening" of our lives.

St. Petersburg, FL

Technological Ecologies & Sustainability, edited by Dánielle Nicole DeVoss, Heidi A. McKee, and Richard Selfe. Logan: Utah State University Press, 2009. 383 pp.

NOTE: The book is completely free of charge and immediately available at http://ccdigitalpress.org/tes/

Reviewed by Leigh Herman, Georgia State University

The inaugural eBook from Computers and Composition Digital Press delivers an abundance of information about the challenges and the heuristics related to creating compositions in the technological age. Of course, digital compositions are not artifacts that can be assessed independently; without complex ecologies—consisting of physical spaces, humans, and computers—digital composition would not be possible. *Technological Ecologies & Sustainability* offers the polyphonic voices of thirty-two authors, in addition to editors Dánielle Nicole DeVoss, Heidi A. McKee, and Richard Selfe, who provide insightful narratives explicating the need to consider and reconsider the ways that technological ecologies are sustained at various academic institutions. Building upon editor Richard Selfe's book, *Sustainable Communication Practices: Creating a Culture of Support for Technology-rich Education* (Hampton Press, 2005), *Technological Ecologies & Sustainability* is heavily grounded in theory, but also loaded with practical approaches to developing writing with new media in the classroom. The book contains seventeen chapters, divided into four sections, which survey the multivariate functions of technological ecologies within learning environments in order to create a mosaic of the issues currently facing colleges and schools across the United States. Each of the four sections addresses sustaining a specific facet of the layered ecologies that comprise digital scholarship; I was particularly intrigued by Section 1 "Sustaining Instructors, Students, and Classroom Practices." The editors of *Technological Ecologies & Sustainability* have drawn upon their rich backgrounds as scholars of both English and computational media to compile the book, providing ample information for a range of audiences from academic professionals to graduate students to professors.

The physical spaces assessed in the book are primarily traditional universities (specifically, state-funded universities). As students and instructors alike rely upon digital devices for composition more and more, classrooms must adapt in order to facilitate these new writing ecologies. In "A Portable Ecology: Supporting New Media Writing and Laptop-ready Pedagogy," authors Kristie S. Fleckenstein, Fred Johnson and Jackie Grutsch McKinney describe the transformation of a set of their English classrooms at Ball State University. They eventually converted their classrooms into laptop-ready spaces, after a few rounds of renovations. These spaces, fitted with electrical outlets for each student, allow for the formation of portable ecologies via student-owned laptops. The authors supply much food for thought, recounting detailed information about the construction process and the backup plans they had to put in place. The authors also illustrate looping models (literally, visual models of loops) for the emergence of change in a technological ecology and link their article to a video which further explains those models. Fleckenstein's, Johnson's, and McKinney's experience provides a thorough logistical analysis of systemic evolution. Their narrative offers valuable advice about updating a school facility; however, the Ball State University renovation cost upwards of $150,000, and many institutions simply may not be able to secure that type of funding.

Anthony T. Atkins and Colleen A. Reilly address the problems of teaching in a technological ecology where resources are scarce. *Technological Ecologies & Sustainability* includes their article, "Stifling Innovation: The Impact of Resource-poor Techno-ecologies on Student Technology Use," which begins by offering a less than sustainable coping strategy for obtaining access to technological resources. Atkins and Reilly describe a professor who has implemented a multimedia project in his curriculum, forced to grease the wheels with "staff members in information technology departments, at the library circulation desk, and, of course, within the Technology Assistance Center" by giving them gifts of "dark chocolates, toaster pastries, cookies, and other treats" (3). Of course, chocolate can only go so far when trying to obtain expensive technology for classroom use. Atkins and Reilly conducted a survey at their university which found that only forty-nine percent of the participants had access to the technology necessary for their coursework, and that this limited access was related to the students' academic self-confidence, especially for females. One highlight of this article, for me, was the downloadable version of the actual questionnaire that Atkins and Reilly used for their research. While unequal access to technology is an issue for everyone involved in the field of education, Atkins' and Reilly's article offers a candid look at how the varying parts of a university ecology are affected by lack of technological resources.

As *Technological Ecologies & Sustainability* unfolds, the editors and authors enumerate the ecologies that arise from human-computer interaction. Although writing centers are easily identifiable as the locus of technological composition within English departments, many different complex relationships are involved in integrating digital writing and scholarship in school environments. In "Political Economy and Sustaining the Unstable: New Faculty and Research in English Studies," authors Rylish M. Moeller and Cheryl E. Ball discuss their experiences as new hires, specializing in New Media, in the English department of a research institution. Collaboratively authored with Kelli Cargile Cook (an established faculty member in the same department), this piece details the trials and tribulations of navigating the political realm of a technological ecology. After frustratedly producing a cardboard sign that read "Will Work for Research $$$," Moeller was able to successfully negotiate for startup funds for his research. And while I enjoyed the humor in this article, the authors produce much more than anecdotes. In the chapter Moeller and Cargile Cook offer a thorough methodology for analyzing departmental politics; certainly, this chapter is a must-read for anyone accepting a new position involving technological research.

Curricular ecologies are also a vital component in this book; multifarious digital composition initiatives have sprung up within the discipline of English. In "Portfolios, Circulation, Ecology, and the Development of Literacy," Kathleen Blake Yancey evaluates how ePortfolios expand the curricular ecology. As President of the National Council of Teachers of English and Kellog W. Hunt Professor of English at Florida State University, Yancey has focused her scholarship on developing twenty-first century literacies. Noting that "an electronic portfolio, with drafts and outtakes and reflective commentary, assembles and articulates *its own ecology of composing and composer*," Yancey delves into three models of electronic portfolios (1). Other curricular ecologies, such as electronic theses and dissertations (ETDs) and video composition, are also assessed in *Technological Ecologies & Sustainability*. These ecologies are all evaluated for sustainability; from the viability of continuing a digital storytelling project in a non-profit educational program to the environmental impact of discarding old hardware, the authors of *Technological Ecologies & Sustainability* pragmatically approach the implementation and development of hi-tech modalities within education.

Because *Technological Ecologies & Sustainability* is an entirely digital composition, the usability of the document itself deserves considerable attention. The book can be either downloaded as a PDF or can be read entirely online through the Computers and Composition Digital Press website. While the PDF is handy for anyone who wants to read without having to be connected to the internet, the book should really be read online. The interactive nature of the text is best utilized by exploring the links and videos contained within; many of the resources that are discussed by the authors (such as www.storybuilders.org) as well as the references at the end of each selection are active hyperlinks. The final chapter of the book includes a video of authors Cynthia L. Selfe and Gail Hawisher discussing their scholarly efforts. In addition to not including videos, the PDF document may cause some navigation issues. The pagination of the book is not the same as a typical printed book—each selection of *Technological Ecologies & Sustainability* begins with page one. This presents a problem in the PDF version because the PDF reader will indicate you are on page sixty-four, for instance, when you are actually on page one according to the pagination of the selection. In the online version, the table of contents is hyperlinked and quite easy to navigate. And, as DeVoss, McKee, and Selfe note in the introduction to the book, by publishing online "the tempo of the interaction between the writers and readers" has been accelerated (5). The editors further this sentiment by adding that "the social networking possibilities of current Web 2.0 technologies will allow the collection to take on a discursive life of its own" (5). As a whole, *Technological Ecologies & Sustainability* is a thought-provoking foray into the rich world of digital scholarship and the logistical needs associated with developing relevant and resonant learning experiences around technology. This book will surely provide scholars of all levels with new ways of thinking about technology in the classroom.

Atlanta, GA

Buying Into English: Language and Investment in the New Capitalist World, by Catherine Prendergast. Pittsburgh: University of Pittsburgh Press, 2008. 180 pp.

Reviewed by Kellie Sharp-Hoskins, Illinois State University

With front-row tickets to capitalism's insidious effects on education, it is no wonder that compositionists are increasingly vested in researching and writing about economies and exchange value in addition to composition, curriculum, and classrooms. The corporatization of the university, diminishing state support of public institutions, and hiring practices that elide benefits in favor of contingent workers demand attention from a field with our specific history and institutional location. Beyond these academy-specific issues, however, the field also has the vantage point and theoretical resources to speak to the complicated connections between language, literacy, and power economies more broadly conceived. At its most basic, Composition is premised on language: where it is used, how it is used, how it is taught, how it circulates, and who has access. And while she does not focus on the composition classroom, these are the very issues addressed by Catherine Prendergast in her 2008 monograph, *Buying into English: Language and Investment in the New Capitalist World*, a "critical ethnographic study" of language use in postcommunist Slovakia (1). Prendergast's argument clearly offers insight to compositionists committed to pedagogy, practice, and more traditional writing-based research, but it does so implicitly. In the following review, then, I offer an overview of Prendergast's arguments followed by suggestions for how they contribute to and complicate Composition's understanding of those very questions that define the field.

Partly attributable to Prendergast's serendipitous post-undergrad employment there, and partly due to its seemingly exemplary status among post-communist Eastern bloc countries in "buying into" English, Slovakia is Prendergast's site to study what it means to invest in English in "the new capitalist world." In her introduction, Prendergast offers the dominant narrative of the history of Slovakia's entrance into capitalism following the "'Velvet Revolution' of 1989'" (2). According to this narrative, English language learning and use was taboo under communism but almost immediately became a necessity following the revolution; Slovakians embraced both the English language and English lessons as the price of admission to the promises of capitalism.

In contrast to this narrative of a "somewhat uncomplicated transition out of communism," Prendergast offers a complex, often contradictory narrative of the Slovakia's relationship with capitalism and globalization. This comes by way of historical and cultural contextualization—for example, she introduces the 1990s as a "period of strong ethnolinguistic and nationalist identification in Slovakia" [following the breakup of a unified Czechoslovakia in 1993] alongside "simultaneous but seemingly incongruous growing appetite for English" (51)—as well as ethnographic triangulation: Prendergast employs multiple firsthand accounts of Slovaks' experiences with, and investment in, English both before and after the fall of communism. Her focus on individual research subjects and their variety of experiences confirm that Slovaks' relationship to English is neither singular nor simple. Though English was officially sanctioned in pre-1989 Slovakia, the subjects of Prendergast's study already had various and complicated relationships to English, and this is the subject of chapter 1, "Lingua Non Grata: English During Communism." Prendergast's detailed accounts of individual relationships to English demonstrate the complexity of its place in communist Slovakia; in chapters two through five, she continues to complicate Slovaks' relationship to English, tracking the relationship through its transition into capitalism.

While English was discouraged, marginalized, and contained under communism, Prendergast explains that "As Slovakia moved toward capitalist integration, it moved as well toward embracing English as the medium through which profit could be generated" (53). But this apparent profitability of English centered on what Prendergast calls "the promise the global economy makes but never fulfills," that of "linguistic fixity" (22). Chapter 2, "Other Worlds in Other Words," tracks this unfulfilled promise by way of Fero, a university instructor, and Maria, an artist, who, Prendergast argues, were "chasing imaginaries of English" initially made possible by Slovakia's isolation from the West in the early 1990's. Both Fero and Maria chose specific dialects of English (British Received Pronunciation and American idiomatic English, respectively) in response to "the unsatisfactory political situation" in the aftermath of 1993 breakup of Czechoslovakia (52). Each found, however, that neither English itself nor the dialect they chose could offer security in the new capitalist economy. The closest Fero could come to the "locus" of Received Pronunciation, the South of England, was to join a labor pool for farm work in Northern England (67), and although he was later accepted into a graduate program at Cambridge, he could not afford the tuition. Despite Maria's command of American English, she found herself nearly starving while trying to gain access to the New York City art scene in the closest city she could manage: Boston.

These obvious limits to the exchange value of English for Slovakians following the Velvet Revolution did not slow its ascendancy to the status of lingua franca. Prendergast argues that it is the image and ideal of English that construct it as a "technologically perfect medium" free from ideological investments (148). In chapter 3, "'We Live and Learn,'" Prendergast uses both pre- and post-1989 English textbooks in Slovakia to evidence the ways this image was created and maintained in Slovakia. She finds that after 1989 "lessons" in English increasingly propagate the logics of capitalism, especially its paradoxical demands of global English users: it is marked both as a *standard*, necessary for all, but also as a commodity to "buy into," capable of providing advantage in the market: "learn me, it beckons, and you will know things others don't. Don't learn me, and you will be the one not to know" (78). In contrast to its paradoxical promises and ideal, Prendergast represents "Real Life in English" in chapter four which, she shows, is about "ranking and sorting," or, like she says later, "borders [and] visas" (108, 148). Her argument culminates in chapter 5, where Prendergast argues that global English is "The Golden Cage," perversely attracting users with promises of security and mobility, meanwhile "add[ing] to their feelings of immobility by initiating them more forcefully into the unbalanced world" (131).

Throughout *Buying into English*, Prendergast emphasizes how English follows the logic of capitalism—it does not, and really cannot, escape the political and economic forces in which it participates. Further, it invites global English users to invest while masking the "deeper logics of capitalism": English "w[ill] always be manipulated and controlled by more powerful players in more powerful countries" (3). Importantly, Prendergast implicates herself in this logic, as a language user and citizen in a more powerful country. She not only acknowledges her returns on investment in the capitalist world as more valuable than those of other global English language learners and users but recognizes her research itself as bound up in the very capitalist logic it critiques. This issue of implication is, finally, central to Prendergast' project of showing how English circulates in the new capitalist world. This book is not an account of how *some* global English users are positioned in relation to capitalism and its language, but how *all* English language users are always already implicated by it. Unlike the image or ideal of English as a "technologically perfect medium," Prendergast teaches us that language is never value neutral, never free from its relation to economic and political interests (148).

In the context of this argument and despite not including a conventional pedagogy chapter (not surprising given that her study and objectives neither begin nor end with language learning in a university classroom) Prendergast's work becomes invaluable to the field of Composition in both the ways we conceptualize language and in what it means to teach English. Insofar that English is not a technology or tool, not a "medium," and never reaches "linguistic fixity," we cannot teach composition as if we are merely offering reading, writing, or critical thinking "skills" to our students. Rather, like Prendergast, we must be willing to implicate ourselves in the complex economy in which our pedagogies and practices, our research, the field of Composition, and English itself exists. We can do this with our students, through assignments that question simple equations of English language and literacy with economic self determination. We can resist framing our English lessons themselves as rhetorical "tools" that serve students without consequence in the larger social, political, and capitalist world. We can follow Prendergast in doing this in our research, recognizing ourselves as beneficiaries of an asymmetrical language economy. In short, we, like Prendergast, must begin to question the narratives that posit English as outside of the global marketplace and insist that composition, as a language-centered activity and field, is always already bound to it.

Normal, IL

CONTRIBUTORS

Heather Bastian is a PhD candidate in rhetoric and composition at the University of Kansas. Her research interests focus on rhetorical genre theory and composition pedagogy, especially the ways in which the two intersect in the construction of reader/writer subjectivity. Currently, she is working on her dissertation in which she examines theoretically how, when, and why writers innovate or follow conventions and tests a pedagogy of "uptake awareness and disruption" that she designed to disrupt conventional expectations and to encourage students to innovate critically so that they can make their own rhetorical choices.

Collin Gifford Brooke is an Associate Professor of Rhetoric and Writing at Syracuse University. His first book, *Lingua Fracta: Towards a Rhetoric of New Media*, was published by Hampton Press in 2009, and his work has appeared in various journals and edited collections. His current research engages the digital humanities, network studies, and game studies.

Kerry Dirk is currently a PhD student in Rhetoric and Writing at Virginia Tech. Her research interests include genre theory, computers and composition, and composition pedagogy. She has published short works in *TETYC* and *Harlot*, as well as an essay on navigating genres for the book series Writing Spaces: Readings on Writing.

Laurie E. Gries is a 4th year PhD candidate at Syracuse University. Her recent publication "Practicing Methods of Ancient Cultural Rhetorics" exemplifies her interests in material rhetorics, research methodologies, and rhetorical historiography. Her current research project, "Still Life with Rhetoric," focuses on developing a consequentialist approach to study the circulation of visual rhetorics.

Bob Mayberry is composition director at Cal State Channel Islands and former editor of *Freshman English News*. He became a teacher in large part because of Paul Adamian. Bob just completed a cycle of short historical plays about the Donner Party and is currently working on a novel about a composition director murdered by colleagues. Paul Adamian bears no responsibility for this latest twisted obsession of Bob's career.

Ben McCorkle is an Assistant Professor of English at the OSU Marion campus. His areas of interest include rhetorical theory, digital media studies, and visual culture. His work has recently been published in journals such as *Computers & Composition Online*, *Rhetoric Society Quarterly*, and *Harlot: A Revealing Look at the Arts of Persuasion*.

Liz Rohan is an associate professor of Composition and Rhetoric at the University of Michigan-Dearborn Most recently she has co-edited (with Gesa Kirsch), *Beyond the Archives: Research as a Lived Process* (Southern Illinois Press, 2008). She has published book chapters and several articles in journals such as *Pedagogy, Rhetoric Review,* and *Computers and Composition.*

Paul Walker is an assistant professor and coordinator of composition at Murray State University. His research interests include composition theory, urban and environmental rhetoric, and assessment of student writing. His essays have appeared in *Writing on the Edge* and *Journal of the Scholarship of Teaching and Learning,* and he is currently working on a book examining the teaching of composition in multi-disciplinary learning communities.

Call for papers

Composition Studies Special issue—Wo/men's Ways of Making it in Writing Studies

Ways in which women and men have placed themselves (and are placed) in Writing Studies continues to be transitional and varied. Still, as Ballif, Davis, and Mountford emphasize in *Women's Ways of Making it in Rhetoric and Composition*, "making it" still means that "[women] hold a PhD; are full professors at an academic institution; are tenured; are well-published; are cited regularly; have contributed a consummate piece in the field; are frequently keynote speakers at national conferences; are actively mentoring other women in the field; are able to have a real life, in addition to their scholarly activities" (7). *Composition Studies* invites manuscripts that respond to the context of "making it" in Writing Studies inside and outside the classroom—in today's economic, institutional, social, and disciplinary climates.

Composition Studies invites manuscripts that:

- explore traditional and non-traditional ways of "making it" in the profession
- historicize women's and men's ways of "making it" in writing studies
- explore cross- and trans-gender alliances in balancing work in writing studies and family life
- explore writing pedagogy and research in the context of "making it" and women's lives
- explore the space of race and/or ethnicity in writing studies, "making it," and women's lives
- explore definitions and contexts of disability, "making it," and women's lives
- explore teaching, parenting and/or "having a real life," and "making it"
- interrogate how the terms that define the field do or do not resonate with men's and women's ways of "making it
- explore ways women mentor and are mentored in writing studies

Format and submission guidelines can be found at:
http://www.compositionstudies.tcu.edu/submissions.html

Submissions for this issue must be in by August 1, 2010 and will be sent out for review. Email submissions and any questions to:
compositionstudies@uwinnipeg.ca

TCU

— Learning —
to change the world™

Offering M.A. and Ph.D. programs in English, as well as a new Ph.D. program in Rhetoric and Composition, TCU provides students with a tradition of excellence in graduate studies that combines intellectual development with practical training and professional mentoring.

Qualities that draw students to our department:

◊ A nationally respected faculty

◊ Competitive, multi-year fellowships and a 1-1 teaching load for Graduate Instructors

◊ Opportunities for experience working for the New Media Writing Studio

◊ An outstanding record of student placement and publication

To learn more about the programs in rhetoric, composition, and literature at TCU, visit us at

www.eng.tcu.edu

www.ingramcontent.com/pod-product-compliance
Lightning Source LLC
Chambersburg PA
CBHW020614270326
41927CB00005B/325

* 9 7 8 1 6 0 2 3 5 1 8 3 7 *